VICTORY

Tales of a Tuskegee Airman

Capt. Les Williams - Pilot
B-25 Mitchell

Les Williams

and

Penny L. Williams

Victory
Tales of a Tuskegee Airman

Books may be ordered by contacting victorytales@yahoo.com

ISBN: 978-1-4502-4480-0 (pbk)

Printed in the United States of America

rev. date: 1/29/2012

Cover photo: left to right: Lts. Harold Hillary, Samuel Lynn, Les Williams, Daniel "Chappie" James. Members of the 477th Bombardment Group at Selfridge Field, Michigan April 1944

Art Walton

To fathers and their children

Prologue

Our family ate dinner together every night while I was growing up. Most nights dinner was rushed because my father held classes in the evening at his dance studio. Sunday dinner, however, was a leisurely affair and that's when he told us his stories.

Most of the stories were about his life as a boy. Sometimes he would talk about his life in the military during the war but usually only if it was about how he met my mother and my debut into the world. Sometimes his fellow Tuskegee Airmen would visit.

The Tuskegee Airmen are the very first African Americans to serve in the United States Army Air Corps and became some of the most highly respected pilots of World War II.

The men who visited were thoughtful, courteous, worldly, and confident men as is my father. Sitting around the kitchen table, sometimes one would say, "Remember so and so?" And the other would answer only, "Yes, those were interesting times." And that was the extent of their conversation about their experiences during the war. Still, you could sense a bond between them that would last a lifetime. It has.

My father revealed himself to me in other ways, like the way he treats his wife and family, the way he handles adversity, and the places he took us to see.

I'll always be grateful to my father for introducing me to the redwoods. These are thousand-year-old trees, hundreds of feet high, that endure wind and rain and fire yet remain majestic. They have been a metaphor for life for me.

I'm grateful for the music in my father's house–blues, jazz, Latin –all of it. I also met Paul Robeson, Kathryn Dunham, the Nicholas Brothers, and many other African American cultural icons of that era.

I'm thankful for the night when I was seven years old and I fell asleep across my parents' bed. My father had left the radio on tuned to Elijah Mohammed and I dreamed I was an Egyptian princess despite my kinky hair.

Just as important is the divine ability he gave me that is the ability to laugh at myself and, thanks Dad, for letting me fly the plane.

The other gift I received in my life from the vantage point of standing on the shoulders of men like my father is that no matter what people say about you, no matter how loud or how long, whether you believe it or not is your choice.

Thinking about my father's place in history, it occurred to me that he was born just a few generations beyond the Emancipation Proclamation. Forty more years would pass before Jim Crow laws mandating "separate but equal" status for Black Americans were overturned with the passing of the Civil Rights Act of 1964 and another forty years would pass before the Tuskegee Airmen received rightful recognition for changing American history.

So much of the history of Africans in America is untold as history books gloss over important milestones. For example, where did the men and women newly freed from slavery go? How did they get from point A to point B?

In our family alone, we have people living in places from the East Coast to Wisconsin to Fresno, California in the late 1800's. Each Airman must have a family story that is unique and revelatory.

No doubt these people who are my ancestors were risk-takers – adventurous, self-sufficient, resourceful, and willing to leave the comfort of the familiar for the unknown; courageous and prepared to be feared and ridiculed by naysayers. Many expressed the ultimate sense of community by being selflessly determined to create a way for others.

Focusing solely on African Americans in the South as history books do is important because the culture is a reservoir of resources. At the same time it allows Africans in America to be viewed monolithically, presenting a limited range of characteristics and behaviors. For many, African Americans are seen as less than human, depraved and threatening.

It should be common knowledge that the demonization of Blacks was promulgated to justify the economic system of slavery employed in the South, however, these stereotypes grew to mythic proportions despite the fact that they are based on fantasy, projection and lies.

These beliefs were still around in the 1940's more than three-quarters of a century after slavery ended. Some people believed that Black men were not suited to serve as pilots in the military—they couldn't operate complicated equipment or make the kinds of tactical decisions required for battle nor could they be loyal to the United States.

An unspoken part of the mission of the Tuskegee Airmen would be to begin to unravel and dispel the myths surrounding Black lives. African Americans spend a great deal of time dodging the untamed shadows of cruel imaginations, removing the mask and lifting the veil in order to live according to their true selves.

Lastly, I can't remember the context of the conversation in which my father recited this poem because I was not much older than ten when I first heard it, but I remembered it and shared it in my high school and college speech classes. The author is unknown.

All men are created equal in God's sight
There is no Black there is no White
There is no high, there is no low.
There is no friend, there is no foe.

The gates of heaven as wide will swing
For lowest mortal or highest king.
The fires in hell will burn as bright
For rich or poor, for Black or White.

For me, this speaks to the vision I see when I read the Declaration of Independence. Despite whatever machinations went on in other men's minds, in our homes we knew this truth to be self-evident.

Recently, my father recorded his life on tape in his spare time or while sitting in traffic on his way to work or some speaking engagement. He's a very active man despite his age. I've transcribed his narrative, an oral history, that appears on the following pages, adding details here and there to provide a sense of place or time, but in the main, these are his words.

1

Ancestors

My grandparents never talked to the children about their lives before coming to California so like most African Americans my age, I believed my grandparents were part of the institution of slavery but that may or may not be true.

In our family some may have been slaves; some may have been the children of slaves and slave owners. Some may have escaped slavery and immersed themselves in Native American life, or some may have been free men and women all along, arriving in America by other means.

American textbooks fail to account for what African Americans did when slavery ended. Many of us have taken stories our relatives told and put the pieces together to make a family history.

It seems as if the people in our family, like many African Americans, just showed up in San Francisco and places like Topeka, Kansas, where my father was born or Racine, Wisconsin, Boulder, Colorado, Fresno, San Jose, or Los Angeles, California.

I know African Americans were there because these are places my family lived during the years immediately following emancipation.

We were a mélange of phenotypes. Some were dark with coarse or silky hair. Some were light with coarse, nappy hair or with soft, fine hair textured like Spanish moss. Some were beautiful or handsome or stunningly brilliant and talented. I came out the color of golden sand and slender like my grandfather Felix.

Each of we four brothers was unique. My oldest brother was the color of yellow gold. Barney was the color of the finest dark chocolate and Ralph was paper bag brown.

According to Uncle Elma, my maternal grandfather, Felix Graves, was from Virginia. Sometime after the 1860's, he left there with a piano, traveling by ship on a four-month journey around Cape Horn to San Francisco. His wife, Susan Clack-Graves, as Uncle Elma told it, left Virginia afterward, traveling by wagon across America over California's infamous Donner Summit to meet him.

When he arrived in San Francisco harbor where Chinese junks anchored next to tall ships his heart must have filled with hope and gratitude. . All manner of men could be found in San Francisco after the Gold Rush.

Felix looked Middle Eastern, his skin the color of cream. My grandmother, Susan, was a softly ample brown woman. Felix was a waiter somewhere in the city, and at one time, they lived on Franklin Street near the center of town.

It may have been a coincidence or the way neighborhoods were shaping up in the city, but Mary Ellen Pleasant lived two streets over from Franklin on Octavia. She was a wealthy African American woman who supported the Underground Railroad and helped former slaves settle in San Francisco. Whether my grandfather knew her or not can never be determined, but Mrs. Pleasant also traveled to San Francisco by ship around Cape Horn.

My grandparents moved from Franklin to Silliman, near the outskirts of town after the 1906 Earthquake. My mother told stories about walking through the devastation caused by the quake and subsequent fires up toward Nob Hill to live for weeks in a tent city.

More than one hundred thousand people fled their homes after the quake. Every park, every square, every plot of ground was covered with the improvised camps of refugees.

Scores of buildings constructed on earth-filled marshes collapsed when the man-made ground temporarily liquefied during the quake. "Never build your house on sand," my mother would admonish her San Francisco heirs in her adult life.

All of Felix and Susan's children–there were seven living–were fair and looked more like Felix except Gordon, who looked white. At the time I was born, my mother had a sister, Ira, and five brothers: Gordon, Elma, Wilbur, Milton, and Clarence.

All of the children chose to marry brown people as a matter of cultural familiarity and personal safety, except Gordon, who married white. Her family never knew he was of African descent until the day of his funeral some fifty or sixty years later. The grandchildren didn't know why neither he nor his wife and child were in family photos or why we only saw them only once a year on the Fourth of July. We missed them.

Everyone in the family carried themselves with straight backs and cool exteriors, concealing hearts that were warm and as big as the ocean. When they spoke, I felt as if I were the most important person on earth.

They moved like cats, deliberate and alert. If a ball was thrown unexpectedly, they could catch it in mid-air from a full, resting position.

My grandparents' house at 1010 Silliman was near the crest of a hill overlooking the bay toward the east. Overhead cables and wires circled the bottom of the hill where the streetcar ran. The brick and dirt street leading down to San Bruno Avenue was lined with rows of houses.

When Grandpa got off the streetcar at the end of the day, one of the kids who had been shooed out of the house would run inside to let Grandma know he was on his way up the hill so dinner would be on the table when he arrived.

My mother, who was born Mabel and later changed her name to Mabelle, was employed at Carpenter's Institute of Shorthand and Typewriting downtown on Montgomery Street. She also taught ballroom dancing, which was to have significance for me as I grew older.

At the announcement of her marriage to my father, the *San Francisco Call-Bulletin* reported that a young white man committed suicide because Mabel Graves was marrying another.

Local historians write that my father, and his father before him, worked on the railroads as chefs, a prestigious position for Black men in those days. Noah Williams, Sr., my paternal grandfather, they write, worked for the Rock Island Line, and his son, my father, Noah, Jr., was ultimately responsible for food services for Southern Pacific's Coast Division. My father never talked about that part of his life. He had a different dream for his four sons.

My father's mother, Elizabeth, wrote in sculpted penmanship in her Bible that she was born in Frankfort, Kentucky. Her first son Noah, my father, was born in Topeka, Kansas in 1888. From Kansas she traveled to Chicago to Oakland to San Mateo, California. When I was older, I spent summers with her in Pasadena.

A picture of a Native American man hung over the mantelpiece in her living room. She might have been married to him at one time, or he could have been her father. At times, she wore her hair in long braids. Her children were brown. Some were stocky like my father and not very tall.

When my father met and married my mother, he was operating a restaurant in San Francisco across the street from the Palace Hotel.

This is the legacy I was born into on August 9, 1919.

Felix Graves

Susan Graves in front of the family home

Elizabeth Williams

**Mabelle Graves seated center front behind
young man. San Francisco c. 1910**

2

Dare to Dream

My parents moved to 1011 Silliman directly across the street from my mother's family home. I was born at home, the last of four boys. My father's name was Noah Cowell Cannon Williams. He named his first-born son Arnold Noah. His second son was named Barney Cowell, then came Ralph Cannon and then me, Leslie. I wasn't given a middle name, so I took one later in life.

Six months after my birth, my family moved twenty-five miles south to San Mateo. My father was opening a restaurant in town on B Street he would call Noah's Cafeteria after himself.

San Mateo had a colored population large enough to support two churches. Also, my father's family had been living there for at least ten years. His brother, Elmer, was born in San Mateo in 1910.

Colored men had their own businesses in San Mateo. Mr.

Henry Taylor had a shoe shine shop on Second Avenue. Mr. Cullen ran a hauling and delivery service and so did Mr. Pickett. Some men worked as redcaps at the train station.

After a few years when this venture proved successful, he built his own place on the corner of 3rd Avenue and what is now San Mateo Drive. The two-story building took up a large portion of the block and is still standing more than seventy years later though it's had other owners and has been through several transformations.

Tutored by a well-known artist of the time who called himself D'Etreville, my father painted 6-foot tall oil paintings of animals he imagined were on the biblical ark and hung them on the dining room walls. Every plate, every piece of silverware; the creamers, butter chip plates, drink glasses and soup tureens, had a trademark picture of Noah's Ark riding the waves etched on them. The tables in the main dining area were covered with white tablecloths. Miniature metal animals paraded around the chandeliers.

The kitchen was modern, of industrial proportions with huge ovens to cook the meats. There was a salad preparation room and dishwashing room and a cellar for storing meats with a chute from the sidewalk to transfer food from delivery trucks.

Patrons entered through a lobby decorated like a large living room complete with grand piano into the dining area. Floor-to-ceiling windows made up the majority of the east wall.

They approached a long steam table to select their meal: desserts first—rice, tapioca, and floating island puddings and cobblers, salads and vegetables next, then the climax with Noah standing there with knife and sharpener to slice the ham, prime rib, or turkey.

Customers slid their trays along the railing then stopped at the cash register where my mother sat. From there the waiters took the trays to a table. They wore black slacks, white, starched coats, and black bowties.

Upstairs, the ladies lounge took up most of the second floor. There was a grand piano in the lounge as well.

"No institution has singly drawn more people to this community than Noah's Cafeteria," declared the manager of the local Bank of Italy. That included African Americans since all of my father's employees were African American.

Some of the waiters came from out of town, and I presume they were men he knew while working on the trains. They moved to San Mateo with their families and established homes. They were respectable, hard-working men whose wives sometimes were employed as servers at the steam table.

There was a small contingent of dishwashers and other help in the back completely out of the view of customers. Mabelle had a small office in the front of the building where she counted the money for the accountant and placed it in a safe that could be seen from the street and was always lit.

In the beginning, we rented houses, two of which I recall were on Railroad Avenue and the front doors weren't more than fifty feet from the tracks. The train station had been the hub of the city for many years with the town growing around it. I recall I did get used to the trains and I was able to sleep through them, and eventually used them like a clock. They always ran on time. The 6:06 meant 6:06.

We had housekeepers because my mother was helping at the restaurant as the cashier and sometimes as a service person behind the counter for desserts and salads. My father arrived at the restaurant at five every morning to light the ovens. Burns covered his shins from lighting those big ovens, scars that would last the rest of his life.

The housekeepers were generally older women. Occasionally, one would have a child who lived with us, one of whom became a life-long friend.

One housekeeper was vegetarian. While my father's cooking was southern, my mother's meals were Californian. In addition to steaks and chops, she prepared soufflés and omelets, a lighter fare with lots of fresh produce.

One famous Thanksgiving dinner when I was five years old, my father stood at the head of the table sharpening the blade of his knife, metal striking against metal in front of the meal our housekeeper had prepared. When he set upon the traditional Thanksgiving turkey his blade cut through the bird without any resistance like cutting through a cloud. Our creative vegetarian housekeeper had sculpted and browned a turkey out of mashed potatoes.

We burst into laughter and although we were disappointed that we wouldn't be eating turkey that holiday, at the same time we were amazed by her artistic skill.

We always had a pet—never a cat, but a dog, parrot, canary, or maybe goldfish. The pets kept me company while the housekeeper tidied the house and Mom and Dad were away at work and my older brothers were in school.

The locations of our houses at that time weren't in the best neighborhood, but it wasn't a dangerous place even though hobos dismounted the trains to sleep under a nearby bridge.

Some of the Mexicans lived near the tracks in shanty-like housing supplied by the railroads that employed them to maintain the ties and rails.

Gangs of truck drivers working for a gravel company in the neighborhood scurried back and forth all day. The delightful discovery of gravel piles became kingdoms for our King of the Hill games.

Noah Williams

The Williams boys

My father's business skyrocketed. His baked hams became famous. Hundreds of hams were delivered weekly into the metal chute from the sidewalk into the cellar.

Many claimed that Noah's was the most modern and possibly the finest cafeteria in the state. In a short while he became a wealthy man so he built a house on a huge lot on Delaware Street.

Dad engaged the best contractor the area had to offer, and it took at least a year to build. The exterior was stucco painted white with a red, Spanish tile roof. The interior reflected the Art Deco period of the time with a stone fireplace from floor to ceiling in the living room.

On the main floor were a living room, formal dining room, kitchen and office. There were three bedrooms upstairs and a bath. We boys had to share bedrooms, two to a room. Downstairs from the kitchen was another bedroom for the housekeeper, a bath, laundry room, and den.

He put in the latest technology with push-button light switches; flush mounted electrical outlets in the baseboards and a pass-through mailbox that delivered the mail directly into one of the front rooms.

In the kitchen two of the cupboards were designed like coolers with grated openings to the out of doors. The icebox was down a few stairs in the laundry room by the back door. The iceman used the back door to deliver blocks of ice he transported around town by horse-drawn wagon.

A mangle about four feet wide for pressing laundry sat on the other side of the room. The room filled with a sweet, ozone smell when clean, damp laundry passed between the hot padded rollers.

We were two blocks further east from the train tracks between First and Second Avenues. Keep in mind, that "colored people," as we were called in those days, weren't allowed to live anywhere in San Mateo, though one or two families did live on the west side, near the tracks.

One large house was given to a woman as a reward for years of service as housekeeper to a wealthy family in Hillsborough. Her name was Emma Collins.

Another family living west of the tracks was the Costa family. Purebred Italian father and West Indian "colored" mother.

One more colored family lived west of the tracks, but they lived on the very outskirts of town on 20th Avenue, which at the time was the southernmost extent of the residential part of town. Further south were dairies, orchards, and ranch properties.

There was no shame living on our side of the tracks. The town was well ordered on a grid system with modest to stately homes, all well kept and landscaped. Streets running east to west were numbered, while the streets running from north to south starting at the tracks were in alphabetical order – Claremont, Delaware, El Dorado, Fremont…. San Mateo Creek ran from the foothills through our part of town east toward the bay.

San Mateo sits halfway down a peninsula, surrounded by the Pacific Ocean and San Francisco Bay. Hills line the coast like a barrier to the ocean. They are a constant, always there, always protecting the city. The western edge of San Mateo rises slowly toward them. The eastern border of the city dissolves into the marshes at the bay shore.

Spanish conquistadors were the first Europeans to arrive at the San Francisco peninsula. They moved south along the peninsula, preferring the warm climate in San Mateo to fog-bound San Francisco for their agricultural pursuits.

We were always reminded of the conquistadors because of the names they gave to our cities and streets–names like El Camino Real and Santa Inez. Our civic center was built around a plaza, and the buildings appeared to be made of adobe with red, Spanish tile roofs similar to the architecture of Spanish California.

The downtown area was bordered by Central Park, sitting on sixteen acres, anchored by the library as majestic as a courthouse, and St. Matthews Catholic Church whose bells tolled the hour.

Our part of town was well integrated with Filipino, Mexican, Irish, Italian, Chinese, Japanese, and African American families. Portuguese lived mainly on the coast.

The water surrounding our peninsula, plump, billowy white fog spilling over dark forested hills and thousand-year-old redwood trees presented a sense of reverence, immortality and forbearance. Looking out over the ocean toward the never-ending horizon, I came to know imagination and dreaming.

I noticed a rhythm in the tides and every now and then discovered a piece of smooth green sea glass, a treasure thrown up on the shore amid the flotsam and jetsam. If I put my feet in the water, was there a boy in China on the other side of the world putting his feet in the ocean at the same time?

On the western edge of town, Crystal Springs Road leads past Hillsborough where the wealthy lived, to Crystal Springs Lake lying at the feet of the coastal mountain range. Crystal Springs Road was a gateway to the wilderness. I didn't have to walk far before the houses ended and there were no more signs of the handiwork of men.

Deer, raccoon, and other small fauna lived in the foothills amongst oak trees and shrub. I discovered lizards there lying on rocks in the quiet heat of the sun. The mere crackle of dry grass would send them darting off.

I admired their swiftness and that presented a challenge to me so I fashioned a way to catch them making a noose from a long, grass reed, long enough to keep me out of the lizard's awareness, casting no shadow. The loop had to be big enough to slip over its head but not so big it would slip over his shoulders.

My quietude had to be superior to the lizard's bearing. I'd still my body so I could hear whatever the lizard might hear. My body suddenly became a universe of blood, nerves, and muscle all working in tune in concert with the lizard, the grass, and the sun.

By concentrating and with patience, I could reach out and slip the reed over his head. You had to catch him by the neck. You can't catch a lizard by the tail because the tail will drop away; he'll escape and grow a new tail later.

I never killed them. After catching them, I held them down, slipped the noose off and let them go.

On the bay side of San Mateo is a promontory called Coyote Point, redolent with fragrant eucalyptus trees. We were told the Spanish brought the trees to the Bay Area to plant as an antidote to fleas. One of the streets in San Mateo is named Alameda de Las Pulgas or Avenue of the Fleas, so they must have presented quite a problem.

A character we called Indian Joe lived at Coyote Point. We spoke of him as the last remaining survivor of the Ohlone Tribe of Native Americans who inhabited the area before the Spanish came. We could never locate where he lived at the point, but every week, once a week, he would ride his horse into town, hitch up to the last remaining hitching post on B Street, and shop for supplies.

The Spanish described the Ohlone in their journals as gentle people, who they observed sitting along with the animals of the region in their circles. I think the Ohlone spirit pervaded our part of the world.

The benign climate and geography, the romance of Spanish antiquity, the soil and the water became part of me. My world was a blend of cultures, geography, imagination, and discovery.

As a child, I often wondered if the land made the people gentle or if the people influenced the land. It never occurred to me that anything would ever change.

3

Community

Many of the colored families who lived in San Mateo proper worked for families in Hillsborough, which was made up of large estates belonging to people who had large staffs with chauffeurs, butlers, maids and nannies. The servants, who were usually colored people, lived in separate and sometimes detached quarters. The gardeners were usually Italians who traveled from San Mateo to work on the estates of regular, established clientele.

Thursday night in San Mateo was always an occasion for colored folks because it was Maids Night Off. The servants who lived on those estates would stream into town. Then you would realize that there were many colored people around. There was a colored-owned club for people to dance and have fun. Later, another club opened on Second Avenue. On Sunday you might see colored people coming out of the hills, too.

There were two churches for colored people, St. James African

Methodist Episcopal Zion Church and the Pilgrim Baptist Church, located almost side-by-side on the same corner of Monte Diablo Avenue. The churches became a hub of activity for folks. Between the two churches was a clubhouse that served as a community center. The Dunbar Literary and Dramatic Club met there and the NAACP. We would have dances or parties there and benefit plays and performances for the NAACP. Most social activity centered on Monte Diablo Avenue.

As a kid, Sunday was always an eventful day for me. Everybody dressed up for Sunday, and about ninety-nine percent of the stores were closed. I was commanded by my mother to attend the Christian Science Church, her church and the church of choice for her boys. My mother was avant-garde in much of her thinking.

Christian Science Sunday school started in the morning around nine and let out at ten and was mostly white. Then I would go to one of the colored churches for another Sunday school.

Sometimes I would go to church service, as church was the only place to socialize on Sunday. I would go to the activities for young people at the Baptist Church or the Christian Endeavor, which was St. James' youth program, held around twilight. That was pretty much the schedule for most colored folks on Sunday.

The colored population of San Mateo grew, due in some part to my father's business. He hired a large coterie of employees–waiters, cooks, dishwashers, and others to staff his cafeteria. A lot of people moved to San Mateo because they had jobs with Noah. His establishment offered financial security and social mobility for many San Mateo families.

I didn't encounter much obvious prejudice for a long time maybe because my parents and relatives knew where to go and where not to go. Jim Crow laws impacted our lives as well. We were restricted in our comings and goings just like in the South; there just weren't any signs to say we weren't welcome. Other means were employed to bar us from certain rights and from aspiring to certain professions. There were no Black teachers, no Black doctors nor were any jobs in retail, auto mechanics, or jobs that required training or mentoring available to colored people.

Still, there was space to move about freely, and we were property owners. Most of the colored people in our part of town were property owners.

Noah's boys experienced gratitude instead, as our father brought a lot of money into the town. Whenever one of us got something, all four of us boys had to get the same thing, so we were a very good source of income for local shopkeepers.

My family spent money freely all around town, though there were some who hated to see my father driving about town in brand new convertible cars with four rambunctious boys in the back seat.

We were trained in manners and taught to honor and respect people, especially our elders. People were civil, or they weren't part of our world. If any white person said anything to shame or dishonor us, my mother would coax us along saying, "Don't contribute to ignorance; don't become part of the ignorance."

We'd circumvent them like children on a play yard give wide berth to the kid they suspect pulls the wings off butterflies and sets cats on fire.

My parents taught mainly by example. My father spanked me with a strap once or twice, and whatever I had done, I didn't do again. We were grateful for our parents, and they didn't think beatings could improve our attitude.

Black men were being beaten and lynched by Whites with impunity all across the country. My mother wondered how you teach a boy to value his own life and to recognize lynching as a crime against his person if he thinks beatings are normal? My parents walked a fine line between raising children with their dignity intact and raising children who fear but don't respect authority.

Sometimes my father would say, "Don't do what I do, do what I say." I would search his face as to why this made sense, and he would have to laugh. This was a source of great joy between us. We adored him.

My father took pride in the fact he lived by *Mother Wit* using the sense he was born with to get along in life. One of the core beliefs we heard most often in our family was to do unto others as you would have them do unto you. This was challenging given my father's daily interactions on the job with White people during the time of Jim Crow but he managed to be civil and optimistic even in the presence of people who considered him less than a man.

His demeanor showed us that though you might see despicable acts or hear vile epithets directed at you, being witness to them says nothing about who you are as a person. I admired his courage: the strength he showed to live out his beliefs no matter what; to come home and just be our Dad demonstrated a sound mind and absolute belief in his value as a human being.

I might point out that when we moved from our Railroad Avenue home to Delaware Street between First and Second Avenue, the area on First Avenue between Delaware and the railroad tracks was Chinatown. The two-blocks were populated with typical Chinese markets, stores, and restaurants.

On Second Avenue, there was a Japanese school attended by the Japanese youth after they got out of regular school. As a child, I acquired many Japanese and Chinese friends—friendships I still have today.

There were four grammar schools in San Mateo. The one I attended was Central School, right in the central business district of San Mateo. There was Lawrence School, mainly for children who lived on the east side of the tracks. There was the Hayward Park School for the southern residents and Turnbull School and a Peninsula Avenue School, both in the northernmost section of town.

There were two high schools: Burlingame High that was all white and San Mateo High School. San Mateo High had as part of the student body, young people from as far north as San Bruno and Millbrae and from as far south as San Carlos and from Hillsborough.

The school had an economic mix. In class, you'd be sitting shoulder to shoulder with children from the wealthiest families in the state or the poorest, but it seemed of no real consequence in the classroom. Outside of school, social standing separated Anglos from everyone else - Italians, Portuguese as well as Blacks, Asians, and Mexicans.

We were involved in many extra-curricular activities growing up to expand our knowledge and enhance our lives, as my mother was quite culturally minded. For example, we'd go to a French tutor after school at Central. We had a music tutor come over to our house to teach us classical music. I started out on the violin and trumpet, my brother Ralph on violin, Barney on saxophone, Arnold on piano. There was a rare time when we all harmonized and played together as the Williams Quartet. That didn't last too long, but it did exist.

My mother had rolls and rolls of player piano music that we would play on the grand piano. There was only classical music. That was her idea of music for us.

She kept a library of writings by Shakespeare, Samuel T. Coleridge, Tennyson, Longfellow, Kipling and Omar Khayyam among others. I fashioned the meter of my poems after Coleridge.

Two doors up from my father's business was San Mateo's movie theater. My brothers and I liked to see the Little Rascals movies. They were like regular kids, except the Black kid who was made to have a speech impediment.

We liked Andy Hardy movies, too. In almost every movie Andy would say, "Let's put on a show!" And he and Judy Garland would set up an impromptu performance in the barn.

Shirley Temple was another child star. Bill "Bojangles" Robinson danced in several movies with her. Children began dreaming of becoming stars in the movies.

I was a little uncomfortable going to the movies with my

brothers. My oldest brother, Arnold, had a big laugh and would whoop and guffaw at whatever he thought was funny. I was glad we were sitting in the dark.

My brothers and I were sent to the Sutro Baths in San Francisco for saltwater baths and massages. Located below the Cliff House on the very edge of the sea was the world's largest indoor swimming pool establishment with six pools of ocean water heated and recycled daily with the ebb and flow of the tides and one freshwater pool. A faint antiseptic smell filled the air like the iodine scent of wet seaweed.

Thousands came to Sutro's to bathe, tour the museum exhibiting artifacts from around the world or attend performances in the concert hall or just stroll and observe. The gallery above the pools sat eight thousand. All of this was enclosed in a glass, wood, iron, and concrete structure painted green to match the color of the water.

Sometimes Dad and Mom sent all of us to Santa Cruz situated fifty miles down the coast for a week or two accompanied by a housekeeper. We stayed in oceanfront cabins across from the boardwalk.

We were given money to spend on rides and games. My father paid for private swim lessons in the pool that was normally off-limits to colored people. We wore swimming caps. That was the concession we made to be able to use the pool.

Occasionally, our parents would visit us on Mondays when the cafeteria was closed. When my brothers were old enough to join Boy Scouts and go to summer camp, I stayed with a Black family who lived close to the boardwalk on Branciforte Street.

Rather than drive to Santa Cruz along the coast, we drove south down the peninsula thirty or forty miles eventually passing farms and fruit orchards, then over the narrow, winding road through the Santa Cruz Mountains. Some cars overheated during the climb and were stopped along the side of the road while their drivers waited for the steam from the radiator to subside and the engines to cool.

Ready for a trip to the shore

There was one serious moment during the drive when we passed the mouth of a road going off to the right to Holy City. We were told to never go near that property because if the people there caught any colored people trespassing, they were likely to hang you.

Another episode from my youth was a particular problem I had with my skin. I had a condition that caused my skin to peel. The skin would peel off my hands and feet about twice a year. I had to wear gloves, as the new skin coming in was so sensitive as to be painful.

My mother sent me to various doctors, healers, hospitals, and clinics. She had me, a boy of nine or ten, riding trains, trolleys, and ferries by myself, going to people all over the Bay Area to try to get this corrected. But it corrected itself, I guess, and by age eighteen or nineteen I no longer had the painful peeling.

4

On My Own

About the time I was 10-years-old, disaster befell the Williams family and many, many other families throughout the nation. The Great Depression hit the land and Noah's Ark, in particular.

Dad had a very large establishment and a large staff, and he just couldn't maintain the restaurant because there was no business. Luxuries like dining out are one of the first things people cut from their budgets during hard times no matter how good the restaurant.

My father was a generous man and had a sentimental attachment to his staff. His establishment was providing an income for many in the African American community.

He kept his employees on salary far too long, trying to help them stay above water as long as he could. It was a huge place. He could have made some economic moves, such as section off the restaurant and employ fewer people, but he didn't.

He couldn't fight the economic disaster rolling across the nation like a storm. His generosity and commitment to his staff were of no value to creditors during harsh economic times. So he went broke.

Though I never heard my parents argue, nor did I ever hear anything untoward about my father, along with that came a divorce. My parents' divorce made the disaster quite complete.

My father lost the properties he owned in San Mateo and investments in Palo Alto. Fortunately, after the bankruptcy proceedings, we were able to keep the house on Delaware Street. My father moved out. My mother maintained that house with us four boys and tried to keep the family going.

She put away her fancy beaded gowns and peau de soie slippers she wore to her parties and traded them for a maid's uniform and sturdy shoes to cater parties for the rich people in Hillsborough.

We'd see Dad at work. He continued in the restaurant business with different ventures on El Camino in San Mateo and in the neighboring town of Belmont, though none of these was quite as successful as the cafeteria.

It was then that I became something of an entrepreneur. That is, I got jobs to help the situation. My mother worked to see we didn't do without, as we were accustomed to having what we wanted. I don't think I contributed enough to provide any real financial relief, but at least I relieved her of buying some of my clothing and accessories.

I took all kinds of jobs—delivering magazines, selling subscriptions to the *Saturday Evening Post* or *Liberty Magazine.* I ran a 9-hole miniature golf course in my mother's backyard that I constructed with felt. The ball fell into a locked box at the last hole and you'd have to pay to get the ball out and play another round.

I delivered newspapers early in the morning, sold candy at Central Park on weekends at ballgames or to people lolling around the park. I worked for a wonderful person named John Pantages who ran a candy shop in San Mateo and had the candy commission at the park. I would do any kind of work a boy of ten could do. At the same time, I was doing what all young people were doing in those days.

San Mateo was a small rural town in those days. Children played in the streets and towns were distinct, some separated by vast, open space. Around 1929 the San Mateo Bay Bridge was completed. It was quite an accomplishment–seven miles long with a drawbridge in the middle. It was the longest bridge in the world at that time.

About the same time, San Mateo started holding an annual floral show. A school chum named Harry Baer and I decided we'd enter the show by building a replica of the newly completed bridge out of flowers.

We made the basic bridge and decorated it with flowers. The flowers quickly wilted, so in order maintain it with fresh flowers, we took a wagon, walking all over San Mateo asking people for flowers from their yards. We told them we wanted their roses, daisies, or whatever they had.

People were very generous, so we constructed our bridge of flowers and entered it into the flower show and won first prize. The prize was a beautiful cup that went to our school. I guess somehow or another we were sponsored by our school but even if we weren't, they took our prize and put it in the school showcase.

I don't know where the cup went from there, but I got to know people all over San Mateo.

As to my high school days, I was always the youngest and smallest in my class. I had skipped so many grades in grammar school I passed my brother Ralph and graduated from grammar school before he did. I entered high school at age eleven.

But I was a shrimp. I liked sports and athletics but just didn't fit in. I couldn't play basketball because I wasn't tall enough. I couldn't play football because I wasn't heavy enough. So I joined the track team. In those days, they accommodated the lighter athletes with different weight divisions – the 110-pounders, the 120-pounders up to the varsity, who were the heaviest. I ran and jumped as a 110-pounder and didn't fare too badly; in fact, I did well.

I liked football so much, but being too small to play, I volunteered to be the team's water boy. When the team traveled by bus from town to town, one of their frivolities that I found personally irksome was being physically tossed and rolled over bus seats by the beefy footballers. They liked to have fun with me, which I didn't appreciate at all.

I stuck with the job despite the mauling on road trips, and I served as water boy my sophomore, junior, and senior years.

My size didn't prevent me from having friends; I had quite a few. Not because of my winning personality but because along the way, while selling papers or candy or whatever jobs I could get, I had accumulated enough money to buy a car.

My first car was a Model-T Ford. I was fourteen-years-old. In those days, young people that age could get a license, so that worked out just fine for me. It made me instantly popular as I could now drive my school buddies to class or outside events. And they piled into the old Ford even riding on the running boards like it was the last boat out of Hades.

It was in high school that I took some of my most interesting jobs. I was only eleven-years-old entering high school, and there were only certain types of jobs available to me, but I took full advantage of them.

One of the weekend jobs I had that I liked very much and I liked the boss, too, was working for Pantages Candy Store as I mentioned before. Pantages had the concession at the ballpark, where the San Mateo Blues played every weekend. Sunday was a big day. In those days, the whole town closed up and people relaxed. A lot of townsfolk spent some or all of their Sunday at the park, so I made pretty good money there.

I had to be constantly alert for jobs because there weren't any regular jobs for boys my age, and there weren't that many jobs open to boys of color. One job I found was working as an usher and selling programs at Stanford Stadium. I became quite a fan of the Stanford University football team.

The best opportunity I had was at the newly opened public golf course at Coyote Point. There was a call for caddies–nothing organized or systematic. If you wanted to caddy, you just went out to the course and waited in line for a golfer to call you. A lot of the young men in town were attracted to this job as caddy because it was the Depression and any chance to make money was taken seriously.

So we would all go out to the clubhouse and get in line. It became so competitive that we would camp overnight before a big golf day. We'd go to a midnight show, then right out to Coyote Point to sleep. We'd build a fire under the eucalyptus trees and camp out.

Going out on a loop, as we called it, carrying one bag got you seventy-five cents—big money in those days. And, Lord, don't be lucky enough to carry two bags and make a dollar and a half!

That was another one of my many jobs. They were all varied, all very interesting one way or another.

Then, for pleasure, I used to have hobbies like raising Monarch butterflies. I raised those at home from caterpillars to flying Monarchs carefully observing their transformations. That was an engaging activity.

I participated in church dramas. The Dunbar Literary and Dramatic Club staged plays for young people to perform in, encouraged by two ladies, Gladys Pettis and Helen Williams. I became a member of the NAACP and helped out distributing flyers for the organization and participating in their benefit performances.

Still, I wasn't old enough to be a Boy Scout. You had to be twelve-years-old. They didn't have Cub Scouts at the time. All my brothers, who were older, were in Scouts. They would go to camp every summer at Memorial Park near the small, isolated town of Loma Mar in our coastal hills.

Instead of camp, I spent some of my summers with my grandmother in Pasadena. That was my father's mother, and she lived at 533 Hammond Street. So I spent my summer days roaming the streets of Pasadena. I had no playmates to run with, but I found out later that a lot of the boys ran with gangs. They weren't gangs in today's sense at all, but I did meet a young man from Pepper Street. He had two brothers, one named Mack and another brother whose name was Jackie Robinson.

Everyone alive during the 1940's and '50's knows that Jackie was the first Black man to play professional baseball, breaking into the big leagues with the Brooklyn Dodgers.

Jackie was my age—just a few days separated our birthdays. I would meet him at Lincoln Park near my grandmother's house. There were recreational opportunities at the park for wayward youth, so I often found myself playing ping-pong with Jackie. Of course, he was an expert in any sport he played. At UCLA he was a football star—an outstanding football player. And in Pasadena, he was a top-ranking tennis player but he couldn't get official recognition because of his color.

I crossed paths with Jackie many times after our summers together as ten- and eleven-year-olds. He went to Pasadena Junior College, and I went to San Mateo Junior College, and we were both on our respective track teams. I would compete with him many times on the broad jump. Of course, there was no match at all. But he was the kind of guy who would help another person do better and give advice. He helped me improve my broad jumping skills, telling me what to do to get better distance. He was just exceedingly helpful. So my affection for Jackie Robinson is endless.

The gangs in Pasadena weren't violent. They didn't carry guns or knives, but they would fist fight. A lot of times, if you were in the wrong territory, you'd have to fight.

I found a better method than fighting. I was small and the

gang members towered over me. To protect myself, I decided to try to entertain them or amuse them by lying.

I would tell lies about a mythical town called Lieville. It was a town so hot you couldn't walk on the street without your shoes sticking in the molten asphalt. I told them lies about all the things you had to do because it was so hot, and they liked it. At least, they stopped threatening to beat me up and instead called me "Lieville."

I was welcomed when I ran across any particular gang. I don't know if I continued that practice of lying. I hope I didn't.

One of the best activities I ever did as a teenager, not becoming a teenager until a junior in high school, was scouting. I finally joined the Boy Scouts. My brothers had all joined ahead of me, of course, and Barney was heavily into it. It kept me busy on weekends and after school, and I didn't have much extra time to get in trouble.

Scouting proved to be very beneficial. I was involved in earning merit badges. I became an Eagle Scout eventually like my brother Barney, who earned close to one hundred merit badges. I earned fifty-six. Two of them later proved invaluable to me in the service–bugling and signaling. I became quite adept at the Morse code and Semaphore using flags.

Blowing taps at Boy Scout camp

I also enjoyed marching and drilling at our regular meetings, which also proved useful later on. I really loved that activity and learned a lot. It equipped me with skills, knowledge, and discipline. The Boy Scout experience helped me later in the military.

There was an incident that occurred while I was in Boy Scouts. We would take many hikes and overnight camping trips. We would usually hike into the hills by way of Crystal Springs Road just beyond Hillsborough.

One time, I was hiking up there with a few friends. Generally, these friends were all white people because I was always the only colored person in my class. It was the same for all my colored friends at different age levels.

We were on this hike, and we passed a quarry. It had an enticing plane, sort of a cliff that seemed to dare us to climb it, so we started to climb the face of this quarry. About one-third of the way up, I got stuck. I was too afraid to go up or down. I was stuck, and I was scared. My friends couldn't rescue me because they were all young and small like I was.

Fortunately, a couple of older boys came by, also scouts. One of them, I think his name was Jim Sevier, tried to rescue me by scaling the face of this cliff. He got abreast of me, and we started climbing back down and I managed to make it down safely. Jim, however, slipped and fell and broke his arm. I was sure sorry about that, but it was a demonstration of how friendly and helpful and comrade-like everyone was in those days. Now, every time I pass that quarry, driving by on the highway, I think fondly of Jim Sevier.

In 1935, the year I graduated from high school, my father took the family on a whirlwind trip to Yosemite National Park. My father really worked hard. He would get up very early at four in the morning and worked all day in that kitchen and in the restaurant. He only had one day off, and that was Monday.

One Monday, he decided he would drive us to Yosemite. He had beautiful cars–a Lincoln at that time–and he loved to drive. In those days, the drive to Yosemite from San Mateo was torturous with many difficult mountain roads to negotiate. I do remember that when we arrived, so many bears were in the parking lot, we couldn't get out of the car until the rangers came and shooed the bears off.

We saw Yosemite Falls and walked up to Bridal Veil Falls. I don't know what else we did, but I know that when the sun went down, he trundled us all in the car and drove us back. That had to be a skillful feat in those days.

I was a good student when I graduated in 1935. Although San Mateo Junior College was right in the middle of San Mateo no more than six blocks from my house and free, I didn't want to go to college then. I thought I would be a misfit. I was tiny. I couldn't have been taller than 5'2". I predicted college would be uncomfortable, so I decided to wait a few years.

A significant turning point in my life occurred during the summer of 1935 when a young man named Luther Smith moved to San Mateo from Phoenix, Arizona. I had never been east of the Sierra Mountains, so anybody from east of the Sierras was from a big city.

If New York was the cultural authority of American life, we were as far from New York as one could go. To me, Luther from Phoenix was like a big city boy coming to our small country town of San Mateo.

Luther liked to dance. I liked to dance, too, but I knew nothing about dancing. He persuaded me to go to San Francisco with him to learn how to tap dance. Since I wasn't going to college, I decided to go along with him.

We'd hitchhike to San Francisco going to many dance schools, hoping that one might hire us to clean their place in exchange for tap lessons.

We finally found a studio that took us up on our offer in downtown San Francisco called McLane's Dancing Studio. It was a two-story studio with 4 or 5 dance rooms and lots of mirrors that we would clean every day in exchange for one dance lesson per week.

At one lesson per week, it was foreseeable that it would be quite a while before we became adept dancers. But we had another stroke of fortune.

McLane's was right downtown between 7th and 8th Streets on Market. San Francisco had a few nightclubs and a number of movie theaters that would have stage shows between the features with big vaudeville stars. There was the Orpheum, The Warfield, The Fox, The Golden Gate…those theaters would host some of the greatest singing and dancing talent the United States had to offer.

McLane was a very generous man despite the one-lesson-a-week deal for cleaning a two-story building. Every day, whenever a great dancer came to town–Fred Astaire, Gene Kelly, or the like, he would give us the show fare and tell us to go in the morning and stay at the theater all day to learn what we could from rehearsals.

McLane was also a personal friend of Bill "Bojangles" Robinson. He was an older gentleman by that time. Most of his career he had danced exclusively on the Black theater circuit. It wasn't until he was fifty years of age that he appeared before wider audiences and in films. Robinson came to town maybe once a year, and he would come to McClane's studio. .

McLane would have his special students come in to meet Bill Robinson and dance for him. Luther and I were included in this group, not by virtue of talent but perhaps of sweat. We were among the privileged that got to see Bill Robinson on a personal basis. He showed us dance steps, and that is a golden memory for me.

We learned a lot more about dance at McLane's than just one weekly lesson. McLane's was a popular place and touring professionals would rent studio space while in town. They would create and practice their routines in his studios. There were great ones and not-so-great ones. After Bill Robinson, the Condis

Brothers were the greatest. So whenever a big shot would rent a studio, Luther and I found that that studio sure did need a cleaning right then.

We stayed in the studio while these dancers practiced until they caught on. A lot of them said, "Look, we'll show you a step if you get out of here." We learned a lot that way.

We thought we were ready to go on tour. We had performed at the local Cloverleaf Club in San Mateo and taught dance at the clubhouse between the two churches on Mt. Diablo Avenue.

McLane said we weren't ready. We'd only been there a year. But no, we were stubborn and thought we'd try the stage, but San Francisco was not the place. It was almost impossible for Black entertainers to work in those clubs and theaters unless they were at the very top of their craft. We were nowhere near the top, so we decided to go elsewhere in search of fame.

We decided to go to Los Angeles. We didn't have all the costumes we needed, we didn't have publicity photos or promotional items, but we tried anyway.

As usual, we hitchhiked. We worked in some dumps. We weren't able to work in any of the nice places like the Cotton Club, so we lived frugally.

Thank heaven for a religious leader named Father Divine. Father Divine would charge just 15 cents for a sumptuous dinner any day of the week. He was our friend. Thanks to him, we ate well.

We never did "make it" in L.A. and I was getting homesick. At the time, Joe Louis was making a picture. A call went out for dancers, so we both auditioned. They took Luther but not me, saying I was too fair skinned. That let me out but I told Luther to go for it. I was going home to go back to school. So that's what I did.

Remember, the Depression was still on, so when I got back home, jobs were very scarce. I managed to get a few jobs, though, before the next semester of school began.

Some of the jobs were backbreaking. I remember working at a wire factory in South San Francisco. I would take the rumbling, lurching Number 40 streetcar up to work. On the way back, the lurching of the streetcar was painful after a long day's hard labor. The straw seats were uncomfortable and unyielding.

I also worked at a car wash. In those days, a car wash meant washing the underside of the car as well, with steam. That was a tough job but one of the few jobs I could get at the time.

School finally started and miraculously, by 1937 I had grown taller. I was breaking into the five-and-a-half foot range. I also let it be known that I was now a dance teacher. I got a few students by word of mouth and taught them at their homes.

I would carry around a portable phonograph and my tap shoes. I picked up a little business—it wasn't too bad. I kept teaching dance throughout junior college.

I liked college very much, and I earned my block letter in sports despite my size by playing soccer. I did well, earned my letter, and so became a member of the Athletic Society.

As I told you earlier, I didn't experience much discrimination in San Mateo during childhood, but after I became a junior college student and made a lot of friends, discrimination hit me full-force one afternoon.

A bunch of my friends, who were all White, and I decided to go bowling. I had never been before. San Mateo had its first bowling alley sponsored by D'Arcy's Sports Shop. My father had spent a lot of money at D'Arcy's over the years, buying sports equipment and toys for his four boys.

We went to the bowling alley, signed up, paid, and I went to pick a ball and prepare to play. One of the staff came up to me and said, "You can't play here. Colored folks are not allowed to bowl at this alley." And that was in front of all my friends.

It was very embarrassing, very disappointing. My friends, however, said they wouldn't bowl either, so I had that little Pyrrhic victory. But I realized right then that San Mateo was changing, and life would be different for me.

My dancing ability proved to be an advantage in college. I danced at noon rallies and became somewhat popular. I got one memorable job because of my dancing that provides a happy memory to this day.

The school was looking for a dance band to play for the senior prom. I guess my 'Lieville' history came forth here, and I told them I had a band. They said, "Sure. We'd love to use you."

As a dancer, I had met a lot of very good musicians in San Francisco. I told them I had a gig for them at a senior prom. The money was good, but the one condition was that we were to be called 'The Les Williams Band' and I would be the bandleader. They'd have to wear tuxedoes. I wore a swallowtail tux myself.

They agreed, so at the senior prom that year, there it was: "Les Williams' Band." I stood in front, baton in hand, making believe they were following every move of the baton. I was elated. We had our pictures taken for the yearbook, and it became a treasured moment.

I had another job cleaning Dr. Alan Benner's office every morning before going to school. That gave me regular pocket change. I liked Dr. Benner, and this is when I took a middle name—Alan. My initials were now L.A.W.

I was also teaching dance on the weekends and started accumulating enough pupils to warrant renting halls and clubhouses to teach in. I had enough pupils to put on a year-end recital.

One of the jobs I had as a regular chore also was working for my father at night doing dishes in a restaurant where he was trying to make a comeback. It was never successful.

Then Bay Meadows Race Track opened in San Mateo and I was fortunate to get a job in the clubhouse as a janitor during the races, taking a broom and pan and sweeping up litter.

In those days, the racetrack clubhouse was mainly populated by the wealthy because you had to pay to get into the clubhouse. The hoi polloi sat in bleachers.

I saw a number of movie stars there, Ginger Rogers, Bing Crosby, Laurel and Hardy, Danny Kaye, to name a few. I would rub shoulders with them, so to speak, at the clubhouse.

What was so remarkable about the job was, that despite paying so little, I swept up gold. I had a pan with a handle, so I didn't have to stoop over, and a brush. Sometimes the clubhouse fans became so inebriated, they would drop tickets to races not even run yet, and I would sweep them unnoticed neatly into my dustpan and run down to the janitors' room to pick out the tickets for the races not yet run.

I would find at least five to ten tickets and, many times, those horses would win. There I was with winning tickets. I couldn't cash them though because I worked there. To solve that dilemma, I asked a waiter at my father's restaurant who looked like he was white to cash my 'sweep' stakes, which he agreed to do for a fee.

I only worked one season at Bay Meadows; however, I made enough money in one season of about three months to pay cash for a good used automobile. I never worked there again, but I'll always remember it fondly. I really cleaned up there.

When I graduated San Mateo Junior College in 1939, I was inclined to further my education, so I tried to go to UC-Berkeley as it was reasonable and not too far from home.

I enrolled at UC as a junior, and I thought I could commute daily to classes, but I was mistaken.

Although I had a car, I still had to cross San Francisco Bay. There was no Bay Bridge at that time so I used the auto ferries. I drove to San Francisco past dairy farms, through tunnels, past oyster huts on the bay to the ferry, twenty minutes to cross the bay, then more driving to Berkeley. It was a grueling commute that up to school and back took nearly half my day.

I tried rooming in Berkeley in a boarding house. My room was so small I could barely turn around, and the landlady served mashed potatoes three times a day – breakfast, lunch, and dinner. That didn't last.

I had set up an agenda that was hard on me because after classes, a couple of days a week and on weekends, I was still teaching dance.

I gave up on UC Berkeley soon after, deciding to concentrate all my efforts on teaching dance in San Mateo. I taught at public halls, renting space from a ballet teacher in town.

My business grew to the point that I needed a space of my own. I rented an empty store on San Mateo Drive for $25.00 a month. It was a small store, but it worked well as a studio. I had a hardwood floor put in and some mirrors. I was all set to teach dancing.

The business prospered, and I continued renting space for a couple of years. But I had clients who couldn't or wouldn't bring their children to me during the week, so weekends I would go to their homes to teach them.

One Sunday, I was teaching a girl named Marilyn Sheridan at her home. I don't recall the time of day, but I do remember the date and probably always will–Dec. 7, 1941. Pearl Harbor Day. I went home in a daze. In fact, everyone I saw that day was in a similar daze.

Young men like myself realized what this might mean. I was twenty-two years old and susceptible to the draft, as were most of my peers. My brother, Ralph, had volunteered for the Army about a year earlier as had my friends Harry Cox and Paul Taylor.

One by one, we were getting drafted, and my draft number was getting closer and closer. I didn't want to be drafted. I didn't want to be a soldier who might get hurt or maimed and be unable to dance when the war was over.

I thought about it and decided I wanted to be in the Air Corps so that if I did get injured, it would likely be fatal. I wouldn't just lose a leg or an arm, but my whole life. It seemed to me to be preferable. So I went to San Francisco to volunteer for the Air Corps.

5
Flight

In those days, the only way to become a pilot in the Air Corps was to volunteer so I went to the recruiting station. I took the physical exam and passed.

I passed the written exam. I did everything necessary to qualify as a volunteer in the Air Corps. The people in charge said: "Fine, we've got all your qualifications, just return home and wait for our call." That "call" never came. *Never.*

At the time I was, however, elated. I went back to my dance classes and told my students I had a good chance to become a pilot. They were all thrilled for me and the very last dance recital I put on in the summer of 1942 was all about flying and all about the air corps. I chose music especially adapted for the theme. I felt I would get that phone call momentarily. I told everyone I was going to become a pilot. I guess I was too trusting.

The War Department completely dashed my hopes. One morning, I awoke to a letter from them. I had never seen an "official" letter like that before, but I recognized it for what it was. It was a draft notice, but not for the Air Corps. I didn't open it. I just left it at the house and made a quick decision to get out of town immediately.

I had read in the colored newspapers that they were training Black pilots, so I made up my mind to go where they were training these pilots and try to get into the corps directly.

I asked my brother Barney to go with me, and he did. He wanted to be a pilot, too. So we made plans to leave town that day. As I told you, I had rented this store, put all this beautiful flooring in and other modifications, so I called my Uncle Milton and asked him to remove and store that beautiful flooring and the other furnishings. In return, I would let him use my car. I had a nice, blue Chevrolet sedan, so he readily agreed.

Me and the car I'd leave behind

So Barney and I left. We got train tickets to Chanute Field in Illinois where we thought the Black pilots were being trained. We were so wrong. They weren't being trained at Chanute.

It was winter when we took the train over the Sierra Nevada Mountains, my first time over that range, and then over the Rocky Mountains. I had never seen so much snow in my life. I wasn't used to seeing snow, much less being in snow.

We got off in Chicago to transfer to a local train for Chanute Field in Champagne-Urbana. We got to Chanute at night. It was snowing all over the place. We went to headquarters, which was sparsely manned at the time, and were told the bad news. No pilots were being trained at Chanute.

There were Black men there but they were being trained as engineers for the planes–planes that the Black pilots would later fly.

They said we could take the Air Corps exam, again, and stay as long as it took us to complete the exam. They told us we could stay with the colored quartermasters who serviced the base, handling supplies, cleaning, and all the menial tasks routine to base daily life.

Their little encampment was way over on the other side of the field's broad runways, so they trucked us over there and we were welcomed. I noticed the entire outfit was Black. Their head officer, a non-commissioned officer, was Black, and he found bunks for Barney and me.

We stayed there. We took the exam, and we passed the mental exam with flying colors. I passed the physical, but Barney did not. He had a kidney stone that prevented his acceptance. We decided he should go back to San Mateo and I would wait at Chanute for results.

I went back to Chicago on the train with him, and that's where we parted. Barney let me have his heavy overcoat, as my California clothes were woefully inadequate in the Illinois winter. I bade Barney good-bye, and I went back to Chanute Field, back to the Black soldiers quarters.

I decided to stay at Chanute until I found out from home of my acceptance letter into the air corps. I guess this was one time that being colored was advantageous. As I told you earlier, this group of colored quartermasters I stayed with was situated way beyond the runways—at least a mile away from the main base. I didn't have a uniform, only my civilian clothes. But the soldiers were great. They kept my secret from the white officers; besides, it was rare for anyone white to visit the isolated quartermasters barracks.

Given loaner fatigues, I blended in. I had breakfast, lunch, and dinner with them. I wouldn't work with them, but I would play with them.

They would sometimes ask me to join their basketball games then I'd eat lunch, play some more and eat supper. I'd sleep in my little cot in the barracks along with the others.

That lasted for at least a week and a half. Whenever a white officer was on his way over, you could see him coming because the base was flat. They had to cross the runways, so there was plenty of time to warn me to hide somewhere. I would hide, and the officers would come over and do whatever it was they had to do, and then they'd go away.

I met some wonderful guys there, but it was just too good to be true. The time came when I was caught off guard. They were going to hold an inspection of the quartermasters, so they told me about it and told me to hide.

I made up my bed, just like they all did, but I made one glaring mistake. I left a pair of my civilian shoes under the bed in plain sight.

So the inspecting officer came by, noticed the shoes and asked, "Whose are these?"

They had to tell the truth. Those shoes belonged to me. They got me out of my hiding place, and the officer was fairly lenient. He told me I had a few days to get off the base and never come back again. So I left, and that was the end of that.

It was still cold weather. I went up to Chicago. I swore these were things I'd never do, but because of my plight I did them anyway. I shined shoes, an occupation too typical for a colored man, but I shined shoes in Chicago. I took all kinds of jobs there.

I worked as a busboy, which came in handy since part of the pay was getting to eat. But I was always part-time. I never got a real, lasting job. I would stay in places so dangerous, I slept with all my clothes on. I slept fully dressed and ready to escape if I had to—it was that bad.

I finally accumulated a little money and was able to rent a room in the YMCA on Chicago's south side. That made life a lot better. I met some Black civilian pilots there—college kids who had learned to fly under a civilian pilot training course Black colleges were offering. I met about three of them at the YMCA, and we became good friends, and one later ended up in the Air Corps with me.

I didn't appreciate their friendship too much at the time because they were always leeching off me. My mother would send cookies, and if I couldn't conceal them well, when they found out about them, well, the cookies were soon gone. They would eat them all. So it was a pretty tricky situation.

However, I did make enough money to write home and ask my mother to send me my dance costumes. I had a feeling I could make much more money if I was dancing somewhere rather than shining shoes and bussing tables.

She sent them, and I'd get my tap shoes and my costume and I would go to various clubs to try to get work. I wasn't too successful, but I did get jobs here and there that paid a bit more money than being a busboy.

What happened next caused me to make another quick departure. I was coming out of the YMCA from my room. I passed the front desk, and I noticed two white men standing there talking to the desk clerk. They were asking for a Leslie Williams.

When I heard my name, I was almost out the door, so the clerk didn't see me. When I heard my name, I just kept on walking. I never went back. I found another place to stay, and my friends brought me my clothes and costumes.

I decided I better get out of Chicago. I was a draft dodger, and they were looking for me. At that time, I was hooked up with a Black booking agent for entertainers and he couldn't have come up with a better job than he did at that moment.

He had a job for me in Indianapolis, Indiana. I was to dance in a show with Lil Green who was famous for her blues tune, "In The Dark."

I gathered my few belongings and boarded a bus for Indianapolis. I got a room at the YMCA there. The next day, I was to be on the program with Lil Green and Tiny Bradshaw's Orchestra at an all-Black club with top-notch entertainment.

While I was there, I got another job in one of the fancy, White theaters downtown called The Fox. I made more money at the Fox than at the Sunset Terrace, but I have to tell you that the Fox was a burlesque theater. It was quite an experience for me to be the entertainer between burlesque acts.

I was making lots of money in Indianapolis, living a life of ease, but that luxury didn't last long.

One morning, I was sleeping late as usual since I worked at night, and I was awakened by the desk clerk who said the mailman wanted to see me. I got up, went to the lobby, and the mailman handed me a letter. It was the very same letter I saw the day I left California. My heart sank. It was the draft letter, but you'd hardly recognize it because it had all kinds of stamps, and notices stamped on it, like "Please Forward" and that kind of thing.

The mailman said, "I can't just give this letter to you. I have to report to the draft board that I delivered it.

"And if you'll notice, the message to you is to report to the local draft board."

So I did. I went down to the draft board, told them who I was, and they gave me two choices: either I could be inducted in Indianapolis or I could be inducted from San Mateo.

Of course, I chose to go back to San Mateo to buy a little more time for myself.

I wound up everything in Indianapolis and got on a train. I re-registered at the San Mateo draft board, and they told me that they would be calling me soon. They still hadn't called me from the Air Corps Recruiting Office in either San Francisco or Illinois. I didn't mind going into the service as long as I could be a pilot.

So I tried other means to avoid the draft. I had another uncle,

Elmer, who worked as a truck driver for a local city government. He was able to get me a job at Fort Mason in San Francisco driving trucks. My job consisted mainly of driving soldiers or supplies down to the docks and loading them onto boats. Apparently the job wasn't considered crucial by the War Department, and it wasn't long before I was drafted.

I was sent to the Monterey reception station where I received the basic issue of gear and was inoculated and indoctrinated into the regular U.S. Army.

Bless her soul; my mother came down to visit me while I was there. That's one hundred miles over rough roads on some very inconvenient transportation. So that's where I started out–at the Presidio in Monterey.

All the men there were given orders to posts all over the United States. I was assigned to Seattle, Washington and given a train ticket.

6

Seattle Cantonment

I rode on a regular commercial train, not a troop train, to Seattle, and it was a pleasant ride. One of the pleasant surprises of the trip was a movie actor on board named Ralph Bellamy. He would go up and down the aisles, and when he saw a soldier he would congratulate him, shake his hand, and offer good luck.

When I got to Seattle, I learned I was to be assigned to the quartermaster corps, which was the inevitable destination of most Black troops who were drafted. Quartermaster meant janitorial, stevedore, or laborer or whatever demeaning title you might have for the tasks we were assigned. It didn't look hopeful.

We were assigned to a military camp called a cantonment right in the middle of the Seattle docks. The 1st Avenue Cantonment was a post with train tracks running throughout it and a lot of asphalt–very little dirt at all.

Sure enough, we became stevedores and janitors and part of a trucking company. That was fortunate because I had that recent experience driving trucks back in San Francisco. That gave me a leg up on most of the privates in our company. I didn't have to sit in the back of the truck where the men were jostled and jolted unmercifully on Seattle's rough roads.

Most of our new privates hailed from Arkansas, and I could see they got very little education in Arkansas in those days.

I learned right away that if I found other responsibilities, I could avoid some of the backbreaking duty we were expected to perform. My scouting background helped here a lot.

If you recall, I had a bugling merit badge in scouts. In those days, they used a live bugler to sound calls throughout the day. I was given a bugle and made the company bugler. That meant I would have to watch the clock very carefully.

I had to wake up the men early every day. I'd blow various calls throughout the day for them to assemble for work or mess. Eventually, I wound up playing "to the colors," putting the flag away for the day then at the very end of the day I'd blow Taps.

In the meantime, I did nothing. I just hung around headquarters or anywhere and just watched the clock to blow the call at the appropriate time. That was fairly easy duty.

I also made friends with a lot of soldiers that had musical, singing, or dancing abilities. We would get together just for fun and put on shows. The musicians were easy to spot, carrying instrument cases from civilian life. The singers were discovered in a more unusual way.

These soldiers were mainly from Arkansas, very few of them from California. Some were from Seattle. What would happen in the barracks at night after lights out and after I played Taps is the soldiers would lie there in the dark and sing spirituals. One fellow would start with a line and pretty soon the whole barracks would join in, maybe fifty people. We got some good singers that way.

We decided we'd form a troupe. Some of the musicians from Seattle knew local girls who could sing. We had a well-rounded group.

There were only a few of us who were educated, and we managed to get the best duties on the post, but we were still privates; however, more fortune soon came my way.

There was only one officer in charge of the whole cantonment. He was a White officer, and he had just gotten married.

When we first got to Seattle, there was what they call a cadre of non-commissioned officers. These were NCOs that had been serving in the Army during peacetime. They were a group of hard-core, Black men with little or no education and pretty rough in their living. They were hard men who had made hard choices.

It was tough taking orders from these men because I remember one of the first times I lined up in formation for orientation. It went something like this:

"Now messers, I wantcha ta line up! An' den when I say 'Right-face,' I wantcha ta pivock on the palms of yo feets!

"Now one of the main things you gon' to do ever'day is read that billiken board because there's things on there printed in indelicate pencil, an' I want you to pay close attention."

That was pretty humorous to us California boys, but we dared not laugh or their wrath would fall on us like thunder.

It was in this setting that this White captain post commander called me into his office. He wanted to stay in town with his new bride and just forget the cantonment, so he asked me—a private—if I would be willing to serve as base co-commander, and he would make me an acting sergeant.

I answered back, "I don't know how to act, Captain."

He said, "O.K., I'll give you the rank."

So I agreed, and that's when I became a Master Sergeant with three stripes on top and three on the bottom.

Then life became really easy. I ran the whole cantonment with my own jeep and all the privileges of rank. I was the one that would direct the evening parade in charge of moving about three thousand men in military formation, bringing the flag down in the evenings, and then sending the men back to their duties.

Here's another instance when scouting came to my rescue. I had known how to drill and how to march, and I listened to the scouts on giving directions to marching troops. So I did very well directing the men in their formations.

I was pretty well liked among the men. My name became 'Sgt. Leslie': "Hey, Sgt. Leslie, will you do this and will you do that?" I was flattered and life was good.

I didn't have to eat the uninteresting mess hall food anymore. I would go back into the kitchen where the cooks would prepare Sgt. Leslie a special breakfast, a special lunch, and a very special supper.

Some of the fond memories I have of my sojourn in Seattle at the 1st Avenue Cantonment, as it was called, were that we were practically in downtown Seattle. I had a jeep at my disposal and could drive off-post whenever I wanted, and I wanted to frequently. I liked Seattle because it was a real city with all the chances for entertainment and culture–concert halls, live theater and stage shows. I attended a lot of them. I remember seeing the harmonica player, Larry Adler, and a concert tap dancer named Paul Draper. I was able to enjoy concerts, art galleries, and other urban entertainments that filled in the 'homesick' gaps.

Another time, the City of Seattle had a scrap metal drive. All the residents were asked to donate whatever metal they had to the war effort. Our trucks picked up the scrap metal.

We would roam the streets, and whenever we saw scrap metal out on the lawn or in the driveway, we'd pick it up and take it to a big, empty lot in the heart of downtown. We carried so much scrap that eventually there was a pile maybe seven or eight feet high covering the lot.

The funny part about it was that the people of Seattle were so patriotic they put out useable appliances, musical instruments, irons, lamps, sewing machines, and other working metal stuff in working condition–that was how patriotic they were.

Unfortunately, our teams would deliver most, but not all, these donations to the scrap yard. Some of the best were kept for personal use in the barracks.

The biggest prize was irons–the men loved finding irons, so they could keep their uniforms pressed and neat.

A lot of other things like lamps and radios started to adorn the barracks. At one time an inspecting group of officers came in and saw our hoard of metal and ordered us to deliver it downtown immediately. Those are the stories I remember most.

Being able to read and write took up most of my time, however. I dreaded paydays. Every month I had to verify everybody's "X" for the men who couldn't sign their names properly. I verified hundreds of signatures, and I would have to write in all these names next to their X.

Another job I had was reading all the illiterate soldiers' mail to them. I read letters from their Arkansas parents and sweethearts. It was a job not to my liking. I felt like a priest taking confessions, as many of those letters were very personal and very blunt. Then the letters had to be answered.

Sgt. Leslie

Our group was still performing. We would entertain in town for many different groups such as the Rotary Club, Kiwanis, and other civic groups, and we became fairly well known.

We got a new assignment at the harbor where Kaiser Steel was building ships. Prior to their christening, there would be a party on-board for all the area Brass—all the admirals and generals and high-ranking officials, and we would play for their dancing. I would sing and dance as Master of Ceremonies, and they were well entertained.

We appeared at a few of these parties when one night I was loafing around the bandstand during a break, and a General Denson came up to the bandstand at about midnight.

He congratulated us for providing such fine entertainment and said, "What do you boys want to be in the military?"

Others expressed their ambitions. When he got to me, I said I wanted to be a pilot. Then General Denson said to me, "Williams, you go to downtown Seattle tomorrow, to the Air Corps recruiting station, and tell them I sent you."

I was there at 8 o'clock the next morning when they opened. Somehow, they had already received notice that Gen. Denson had sent me to see them. I was hustled through as if I was getting the red carpet treatment. And I was. Finally.

Before I knew it, in the next couple of days I was on a train going to Tuskegee for pilot training.

My departure from camp was memorable. Our honeymooning captain had to come back to take over his old duties. Like I told you earlier, our camp was full of railroad tracks running right through the camp along the way to other destinations, so the train that was to carry me off to Tuskegee ran right through our camp.

I happened to leave at noontime when most of the soldiers were there for lunch. It was a moving moment because the train had a platform on back like the ones for whistle-stopping politicians, and I stood on that platform waving as the train pulled out to all the men who had become my very good friends. And that was the end of my soldiering career.

Incidentally, at the time I left for Tuskegee, the whole camp had been reassigned to duty in Alaska.

I was allowed a couple of weeks layover in San Mateo before reporting to Tuskegee. That was nice for my mother because she had two sons who were going to be away to war. Like Barney who had the kidney stone, our oldest brother, Arnold, was too old to be drafted so he didn't have to be concerned with military service either.

My mother joined the American War Mothers through one of the African American churches and planted a victory garden, as they were called, to keep eating well while America was put on rations.

I was pleased to learn that my uncles Milton, Elma, and Gordon had done a fine job of storing my dance flooring of beautiful birds-eye maple, and that Milton was keeping my car in good condition. That gave me a lot of comfort.

I didn't have a girlfriend to leave behind, and I certainly didn't have any business getting one. I was U.S. Government property. So I was anxious to get on that train and see what was in store for me at Tuskegee.

7

On My Way

I had a first-class ticket, I guess because I was a Master Sergeant, straight through to Tuskegee.

Near my time to depart, I went to San Francisco to this huge depot. Trains were the most common form of transportation in those days. While waiting for my train to arrive, someone said, "Do you want to get there a little faster, Sergeant? There's a troop train leaving momentarily."

I said, "Maybe I do."

I went down to the troop train, started to board with my barracks bag, and I noticed the train was full of soldiers who were all white and who quieted down as I entered the car and gave me all sorts of very inquisitive looks.

It didn't take me long to realize this wasn't my way to Tuskegee, so I got off the train and waited for my original train to come.

I had never traveled first-class any real distance on a train, and I was anticipating a nice, comfortable journey. I had breakfast in the dining car with the rest of the passengers and awaited our arrival at El Paso. Everybody was told they would have to change trains. Other things were about to change, too.

We got to El Paso. I was carrying my barracks bag, and I went to the large station lobby, waiting with the other passengers for further instructions from the loudspeaker.

I noticed a colored porter as I was standing there, who was sweeping trash. He came up to me and began feverishly sweeping at trash that wasn't there.

He kept his head down and said to me, "Soldier, you're not supposed to be in this waiting room.

"You're supposed to wait in that room over there." And he pointed. I saw the sign above the entrance that said, "Colored Passengers".

I knew what he was talking about. I had never actually experienced segregation before, so I just stayed where I was. I figured I was a Sergeant First Class with a first class ticket, so I should travel accordingly.

When the train came along and it was time to embark, I noticed that the colored passengers on the platform were heading down toward the front of the train near the coal cars. The rest of the passengers were ushered to cars more distant from the coal cars.

I also realized that was where they expected me to go. But I was determined not to. As I was walking down the platform I saw a colonel walk by, so I dropped into step with him and started chatting. I talked about the nice weather, our destinations and what-have-you, and as we walked, we passed the point where colored passengers were to embark.

I walked right by the conductor who stood separating the

races, and I stayed with the colonel who never did reply in our one-sided conversation, and I boarded the whites-only car. And the colonel went on his merry way.

This was the long part of the journey that comprised a couple of days. I kept riding First Class and eating first class with no incident. Nobody challenged me—not one incident whatsoever.

The next stop was New Orleans, and I had been told, as had all other passengers, that we were to change trains again. Not only did you change trains, you changed stations.

The incoming trains we were on would stop on one side of New Orleans and all the passengers going to, let's say Alabama, had to go to the other end of town to a station that served southern destinations.

I got off the train in New Orleans with my barracks bag and boarded a streetcar. It was at the beginning of the line, early in the morning, and the streetcar was empty. I got on, sat down in the front seat, and we proceeded from the station into a residential section of town.

The conductor asked me to move back a seat as the car took on passengers. I noticed a sign over the second seat reading "For Colored Only".

We got to another stop, some more white passengers got on, and the conductor asked me to move back another seat and to take the sign with me. So I did, and I hung the sign over the next seat. And we got to a more thickly populated section of town, and the car filled up. I had caught on by now, and I moved back and put the sign farther back

Needless to say, when we got across town, I was standing in the rear of a very crowded streetcar with a sign in my hand reading "For Colored Only".

When I boarded the next train, there were no tricks I could pull to avoid traveling in the colored car. They were very emphatic about where I should go, and I wasn't about to create a disturbance in such a strange land. So I traveled in the colored section, through Louisiana, the western part of Mississippi, into Alabama and on to Tuskegee.

That wasn't so bad, but it was the first time I had to eat behind a black curtain. When I went into the dining car to eat, I was placed at a table at the end of the car where a black curtain was pulled around me. I was hungry, so I ate under those conditions.

I noticed that when we pulled through towns or stopped for water, or even slowed through town, that the Black children out at the tracks knew where the colored passengers were eating, and they would come to my window and wave and shout and then we'd move on.

We eventually got into Alabama at nighttime. We came to a train stop called, "Chehaw". That was where I was to get off. I knew that because on the way to Tuskegee I met an Air Corps officer, a fellow with blond hair and blue eyes who turned out to be colored. His name was Romeo Williams. He had just graduated Tuskegee, earned his wings, and was returning from a visit home.

He gave me an idea of what to expect, told me I would be getting off at Chehaw, told me I might expect some unusual treatment from the other colored cadets, but he didn't tell me too much else. But he was a very nice guy.

When I got to Chehaw, his stories took life. I stepped off the train, first, into a huge puddle of water, and got mud all over my uniform. Some soldiers came up and told me a truck was being sent for me from Tuskegee. I got on the truck, so did Romeo, and we went to Tuskegee.

I don't remember the first impression I had of the place, but I wound up in a barracks occupied by Black cadets all wearing the same blue jumpsuits. They were all very excited about my arrival. They were there to greet me, but I guess that depends on what greet means.

As soon as I got into the barracks, they took my bag away and took my hat off. They sat me down in a chair, threw a cloth over my chest, like in a barbershop, and before I knew it, they shaved all the hair off my head.

I learned these were my upperclassmen, but they weren't too far 'upper'. There was only one class ahead of me. I had nine months to go as a cadet.

It was a hectic first few days. As time went on, it didn't get any better, but I began to understand the rules and how to play the game. The game was: if you were the newest cadet, you were subject to all kinds of hazing and harassment by upperclassmen.

Classes were ranked in three categories: the incoming cadets in what was called Primary Training, those who had been there three months in Basic Training, and those who had been there six months in Advanced Training.

The incoming cadet was subject to hazing from both the Basic and Advanced groups. Hazing occurred every day of training.

One of the worst physical hazings I underwent as a cadet

came at the hands of Daniel 'Chappie' James. Chappie's class, 43-G, came through our quarters hazing us in 43-J. Chappie had us stand at attention, then called us out one-by-one. One of my classmates responded sarcastically. Chappie turned around and asked everybody, "Who said that?" Nobody answered.

He said, "Well then, you did it, Williams. I'm coming back at the end of the day, and what I do to you will make you admit to making that remark."

I went through the day, and he came back into our barracks as promised. He had me do very strenuous maneuvers. I did them all because I wasn't going to squeal on the guilty party; besides, I really didn't know who made the comment.

He put me through maneuvers at great length. I was dripping wet with sweat and becoming exhausted. He just kept punishing me, going through one exercise after another, all very physical and straining on the body.

He kept asking me to confess. I never did. Eventually, it came time to go out into evening formation, so he left. I was wet and sore. With difficulty, I put on clean clothes.

I ran out of the barracks to join formation. There were steps outside the barracks, and when I stepped down, my legs buckled with fatigue. I fell flat on my face and had to pick myself up to get into formation.

I thought what he did was improper and uncalled for and that he had a mean streak in him.

We were there at least a month before we even got near an airplane. We were too busy with ground school, learning about paper work, navigation, calculating distance and times, and how to read the weather and the theory of aerodynamics.

We were really burdened with bookwork. That kept us very, very busy until they finally took us down to the "line," which was the area in front of a hangar, and introduced us to our first group of flight instructors.

Our instructors were Black civilian pilots who had come from all over the United States, and they introduced us to flying.

I remember my first day on the line. They had my group come down and stand by the plane—a Stearman that was a primary trainer. The Stearman had cloth wings. I clearly remember the first sentence out of our trainer's mouth:

"See that? That's an airplane, and it can kill you!"

I'll always remember that sentence.

8

Tuskegee Institute

The military awarded the U.S. Army Air Corps contract to Tuskegee Institute to train America's first Black military aviators because Tuskegee already had an airfield and a proven civilian pilot training program.

We would have to meet the same standards as any other air cadet. We were training to become pilots at Tuskegee. Others were being trained around the country as officers in operations, meteorology, intelligence, engineering, or medicine.

To complete our segregated squadron, enlisted people were trained to be aircraft and engine mechanics, armament specialists, radio repairmen, parachute riggers, control tower operators, policemen, administrative clerks, and all the other skills necessary to function as a fully self-contained unit.

We were housed in dormitories on the campus. That was nice in that we were able to mingle with the students. We ate in a very elegant "mess hall" as we called it, but it was actually the student dining room.

Jiggs and me in front of the "Mess Hall"

We were quartered two to a room. I had the misfortune of being paired with a man named Eugene Smith. He was a young married man who had been in college but was having marital difficulties. In the room where we were to study and prepare for the next day, Eugene kept me up all night describing his marital woes and asking my advice. I never got a decent chance to study all during my primary training. I had a miserable time with Eugene.

While we were in primary training, we didn't go out to the Tuskegee Airbase. We went out to train at a place called Moton Field. Moton was a dirt field with a single hangar far enough away to require a bus ride from our company area.

Every morning, we would be bussed out to Moton Field when we did start to fly and, at the end of the day, bussed back to the dorms to study and prepare for the next day.

A lot of the fellows in my group had already flown in civilian college programs, but I hadn't. One of the big expectations for everyone was that once we had taken our orientation ride some of us would throw up over the side of the plane because of our greenness.

I'm proud to say that I went up, and while I was excited, I didn't throw up. There were some who did who were allegedly experienced flyers.

Our class was called 43-J, meaning we started in 1943. Every class had to have a class captain, and my class chose me. I like to think it was due to my experience as a master sergeant, and I might know a little more than the average person about the army.

The bus to take us to Moton Field

Or maybe I was elected class captain because I was the only one dumb enough to accept responsibility for such a diverse group of characters. We were from all over the United States, north, east, south, and west, and difficult to command. Each had his own experience with varying degrees of discrimination depending on what part of the country he was from. Each had his own way of maneuvering and coping with a racially charged environment.

The class I was in was comprised of nonsoldiers. They were no more interested in learning drill, right faces, or forward march than they were interested in becoming civilians again. They wanted to be pilots.

I found out what a small world this is though. A lot of my acquaintances prior to coming into the air corps were people whose desires paralleled mine. Like when I went to Chicago as a draft dodger, I had met Black men who had prior civilian flight training. One was named Henri Fletcher, and sure enough he was in my class.

At Chanute Field where I first sought to become a pilot and where I was sheltered by the Black soldiers quartered way at the end of the runways, one of my "hosts" had become a communications officer at Tuskegee who instructed a part of our primary training.

When I was initiated into the air corps with my haircut, one of the observers was Jiggs Thomas from Los Angeles who had soldiered with me in Seattle. I don't know what became of Romeo Williams.

Of course, we didn't start out flying. We started with ground school.

As class captain, I had to see that everyone made formation on time and kept the company area clean. I had to make sure they reported to classes on time and be a kind of father to them.

It proved to be a challenge because we were kept busy all the time going to classes and preparing for classes, harassed daily by upperclassmen who put us through their petty tortures. We had to cope with it all.

Add to this all the duties of cadet captain and you have a recipe for a grueling schedule. The only relief came with sleep. Ironically, it is a time I treasure.

I recall our daily activities included getting up around 5 a.m. and being turned over to our physical education instructor, Sgt. Sableaux, who would have us run in the dry arroyos of Alabama rivers. Even at five or six in the morning, it was hot.

If we didn't go for a run, we did vigorous exercises that we begrudged but kept us in excellent physical shape. I bet we could have stood on one finger if we had to.

Of course, the main topic was flying. The main goal of all who came was to stay in the program.

One of the ways to stay in and not wash out was to solo your plane within a specified time. I personally had difficulty getting to solo because I had to convince my flight instructor I was ready.

His name was Stevens. I was frustrated, so I asked him what the matter was. He told me I was too cocky at the controls and that's why he was keeping me grounded.

All around me my classmates were flying solo, and those that didn't do well were scheduled for a check ride, a real tough ride given by a white officer named Capt. McGoon.

McGoon would fly these fellows to find out why they weren't soloing, and if they didn't fly up to his expectations, they were eliminated or washed out.

There proved to be many ways to wash out throughout training and beyond. This was just the first hurdle cadets had to overcome.

Because my Black instructor wouldn't permit me to solo because he felt I was too cocky and overconfident, sure enough, I had a '"check ride" scheduled with Captain McGoon in the morning.

All that night, my classmates sympathized with me because rarely did one pass a check ride with McGoon. They said, "Capt. McGoon had him a coon." And that coon was doomed.

The next day, I strapped on my parachute and waited for Capt. McGoon to come down to the flight line, and he did.

I climbed into the plane, and he got in the back seat. We were flying an open-air cockpit Stearman P-17. He told me to take it for a ride.

I was very nervous and sweating from more than the heat. But I took him up. We did a few maneuvers then he asked me to land. I landed a good distance from the hangar, so I was preparing to taxi him over to the hangar but he got out and said, "No, I'll walk back. You go ahead and take her up."

Wow, I passed!

That was one of the most exhilarating moments of my life: my first solo flight. When I took off, I'm sure I could be heard over the engine yelling with excitement. There I was in the air. I was flying solo. My confidence grew. I don't know if I was cocky or not, but I felt cocky. I had brought her home safely, and I was one of the boys.

I was still in primary training and had a little more to do, such as proving I could fly cross-country, that I could navigate from point A to point B without deviating, and that I was a capable pilot in general as far as the PT-17 aircraft was concerned.

When we reached phase two, which was basic training, we moved from our university quarters to the Tuskegee airfield where all the facilities of the Army Air Corps were installed–huge runways, great training devices, and lots of hard work.

I was re-elected class captain, and we got into flying the basic trainer. In basic training, our instructors were actual Air Corps pilots, all white, with varying degrees of self-discipline. It was at this stage of our training that everything changed and racism became part of our daily experience.

These Air Corps pilots weren't there because they looked forward to training Negro pilots. They were there because it was a guaranteed promotion. If they would endure living in close quarters with Negro troops, they would get an automatic raise in grade from lieutenants and graduated to captains and so on.

The racism manifested itself in mistreatment. If we didn't do what they wanted us to do exactly the way they wanted us to in the plane, this stick in the middle that steered the plane was rattled around your knees and legs mercilessly because there was no way to avoid it in the cramped cockpit. Your knees really got worn out and black and blue from the beating.

They demeaned us further by using the "N" word. They would pronounce nigger in so many different ways that you couldn't mistake their meaning. But it was one of those things that we absorbed as just a part of all of the hazing though for some, it summoned tears of anger and frustration.

We were determined to graduate and get our wings, so we grit our teeth. They stretched our patience beyond the limit. Still, we were determined.

A lot of washouts occurred during basic training. I don't know the exact number, but our class came in as forty or more, and at basic we were but twenty or more. So a lot of us washed out along the way–good pilots, too.

It had nothing to do with talent, knowing how to fly, but everything to do with the White officers perceptions as to character or lack thereof. You had to make sure not a hint of anger or resentment showed on your face despite the names you were being called. "Attitude" washed out many a capable pilot.

Those who washed out had our sympathy, but throughout our nine months of training, we were always aware that Black pilots from Tuskegee were fighting for Uncle Sam in North Africa, Italy, Hungary, and Germany.

We always got word of how they were doing, who did what or who got killed. White bomber pilots had begun requesting our fighter pilots, known as the Red Tails because they painted the tails of their P-51 Mustangs red, when they learned we never lost a plane that we escorted into enemy territory.

The white officers also used divisive tactics, trying to get us to betray one another. For example, as the cadet captain, I was called in to the C.O.'s office and, in the presence of the commandant and other officers, I was commanded to investigate my classmates for potential communist leanings. This was outrageous. But I had learned how to play the game.

I said, "Yes, I will investigate for you." I saluted smartly and left. Of course, I didn't. There was no reason to.

So I went to report back as ordered, and I said to the C.O., "Sir, I could find no evidence of communist leanings among my classmates, sir."

In basic training, flying got a little more exciting. We were doing war maneuvers, and the planes we flew now had retractable landing gear that allowed a good deal more air speed. We did a lot more instrument flying and things that were more practical for combat flying.

At this point, my scouting experience came through yet again. We began to use the radio quite a bit, and a lot of the messages we sent and received were in Morse code. I had learned Morse code in scouting and it really helped me easily master that part of my flying career.

Captain Williams

At Tuskegee Airbase, we shared airspace with the advanced cadets as well as those graduates who had already received their wings and become officers. They were doing their tactical training, so you really felt you were part of the war machine.

We weren't neglecting other things now that we were flying, specifically, physical fitness.

Every morning, we'd have to get out and run in that hot Alabama sun at least four miles under the supervision of Sgt. Sableaux, who ran with us so we couldn't shirk.

Then we were busy with other things such as using a stationary device to learn instrument flying. You got in a little box called a Link Trainer and simulated flying. That required exacting discipline to master but it was all for our own benefit.

Things were getting very exciting, and soon I was flying in Advanced Training, the last class before you would become an officer.

There, we flew yet a faster plane called the AT-6. We were practicing aerobatics quite a bit in the old AT-6. It was then that I learned I was not suited for fighter pilot training.

We'd practice solo, and one day I was practicing loops and dives. It was in a dive, I learned of the danger I posed to myself. It was in a dive that I passed out.

The plane had a way of righting itself, completing the dive, and when it had returned to the altitude that my dive originated from, I came to at the same altitude, as if I hadn't begun a dive at all. That was very scary and very, very dangerous.

So I found out I couldn't dive without passing out. It wasn't a momentary thing. It had something to do with my sinuses. But all was not gloom and doom. A virtual miracle occurred for me then, and it came from Washington, D.C.

The War Department decided that they were going to let Negroes fly bombers. I guess that was based on the fact that the

Black fighter pilots were doing so well overseas, making a name for themselves as the Fighting Red Tails.

They happened to institute this program at the exact time I thought my Air Corps career was over.

They told our class, 43-J, in the middle of our senior program that any of us who wished to switch over to bomber pilot training should do so.

Mainly initiated for the benefit of tall, big men who had a hard time in the confined cockpit of a fighter plane, the directive seemed heaven-sent. I volunteered right away.

Our class was the very first class of bomber pilot cadets. There were nine of us to volunteer. We abruptly stopped our fighter training and switched over to bombers. That meant we would start flying trainers with two engines. That was a difficult transition indeed as we flew a BT-10, I think, a very light plane with a tail wheel. Tail-wheeled planes are always hard to land and to fly.

Somehow we made it—all nine of us. I was the class captain again, and when we graduated in November 1943, we were the very first group of black bomber pilots ever commissioned by the air corps. That is quite a distinction.

It took a particular kind of courage to fly a bomber because you had to fly straight into anti-aircraft and low level skip bombing required you to fly as low as five hundred feet over the targets.

The other members of our class graduated as fighter pilots, but nine of us became bomber pilots and I was glad because bombers don't dive at the rate that fighters do so I wouldn't be plagued with the problem of blacking out.

I stayed in the Army Air Corps as a pilot as I always wanted.

First Bomber Pilots Receive Wings at Tuskegee

Members of the first class of twin-engine pilot trainees to receive their wings and commissions as second lieutenants, who were graduated at the Tuskegee Army Air Field Wednesday and, after a short leave of absence, will undergo transitional training in B-25 (Mitchell) Medium Bombers at Mather Field, Calif. They are, left to right: 2nd Lieutenants Herman R. Campbell, N.Y.C.; Hemry F. Fletcher, San Antonio, Texas; Perry Hudson, Jr., Atlanta; Vincent J. Mason, Orange, N.J.; Haldane King, Jamaica, N.Y.; Jerome D. Spurion, Chicago; Harvey N. Pinkney, Baltimore; William D. Tompkins, Fall River, Mass., and Leslie A. Williams of San Mateo, Calif. Lieutenant Williams stood first in the class and Lieut. Pinkney, third.

The Black press follows the Airmen (*Williams far right*)

9

Campus Life

There wasn't much social life at Tuskegee, particularly during the time we stayed on campus as cadets. We were so busy doing our homework that we just didn't have time.

We never got any real time off base. When I did, I made it a point to see what the town of Tuskegee was like. Town was six or seven miles away from the campus. We called it White Tuskegee.

I went to town by myself. I had been warned about the sheriff who maintained law and order in town. He was known as Two-gun Pete because he carried two guns with him.

The story was that treatment of Blacks was disturbing, to say the least, so I went on my guard. I noticed very few Black people on the sidewalks and very few Black people in the stores. I didn't even bother going into a store to face discrimination on their turf.

I did decide to go to the show. There was a movie I wanted to see, so I went in the afternoon.

I bought a ticket, and I noticed that it was a one-audience one-screen theater, but it had a large cloth divider dividing it into white and black sides. I, of course, sat on the Black side. You could tell which side to go to without even opening your eyes because you could hear this "pop, pop, popping" and snap, snap, snapping of the people on the Black side chewing gum. They chewed so loudly it sounded like a field of crickets. After the show, I went right home. White Tuskegee had nothing for me.

Most my off-hours were spent exploring the campus. It was a beautiful campus. We ate with the student body in a pretty and spacious dining room that in my view was majestic.

They also had a beautiful chapel and a statue of Booker T. Washington, the mentor of Tuskegee. There were some shops I liked. A beautiful girl ran the photo shop, so just about everyone in our outfit had their picture taken just to be in her presence. The student body was sizeable.

One sad story was that they had a wonderful marching band, and the bandmaster's son was a Tuskegee air cadet. Unfortunately, while I was there, he was killed on a training mission. It was a somber campus. The parade grounds were silent for quite a while.

The main off-campus activity took place in a block of businesses immediately outside campus known as 'The Block.' There was a post office, a small men's store, and a few other small businesses I don't recall. These Black-owned businesses catered to the students. I hung around the block quite a bit, but it wasn't too interesting.

When we entered the next phase of training, basic training,

and left the campus to be quartered at Tuskegee Airbase instead of Moton Field, it was a little more interesting there as far as contact with the opposite sex was concerned.

Although white officers ran the airbase, all the departments had either civilian workers or soldiers staffing them. For example, the parachute riggers were all Black women. They were young girls and very attractive.

There was also a group of WACS that performed the jobs assigned to women although we didn't associate with them too much for ethical reasons. When you became an officer, you definitely didn't associate with them because you couldn't consort with enlisted personnel. After becoming an officer, some of the cadets got married.

The girls were interesting companions, so life wasn't too bad when the girls became part of the experience.

10

The 477th

I graduated in November 1943, Class 43J, and received my wings and bars. I was a full-fledged officer and a gentleman. The prejudice against us, however, would become more highlighted with our success.

After graduating from Tuskegee, our first assignment as bomber pilots was at Mather Field, California, on the outskirts of Sacramento. Nine of us were assigned to advanced tactical training at Mather Field about three hours drive at the time to San Mateo. I could see going home on weekends.

We were assigned to a part of the post dedicated to the B-25, known as the Billy Mitchell. The B-25 is also known as the bomber that surprised the Japanese on their home territory and was depicted in the movie, "30 Seconds Over Tokyo".

It was a great airplane and a safe airplane. We couldn't have been assigned a better plane or better duty. So we made our preparations to go to California.

Me and co-pilot Bill Rucker

B-25 (Mitchell) Medium Bombers flying formation

By the time we were to report for duty, I had gone back to San Mateo to pick up my car that Uncle Milton had taken such good care of.

I had been telling my companions, "Now things are really going to be nice. You're coming to my home state of California, and we don't have prejudice there." I was very wrong.

When we arrived at Mather Field, everything was fine as they accepted us and registered us and assigned us to barracks. We were quartered along with white officers. We ate with everyone else in the same mess hall. I remember a very marvelous Thanksgiving dinner. I still have the menu.

Soon, an inspecting general passed through Mather. We all passed before him in review. The Black officers were interspersed throughout the parade. Some were very big men, though we all looked like typical trainees.

We passed by the reviewing stand, and the general noticed that some of the heads looming above the rest were Black trainees.

He apparently didn't like that. The very next day, things were drastically different. We were told we couldn't eat anywhere in the officers mess but were emphatically directed to sit at a separate table designated just for us.

It was a round table with nine chairs. I don't recall if there was a sign on it, but we were told that was the only place we could eat in the mess hall.

So we never ate at the table. Never! We managed to get through the day eating elsewhere, and at night we could eat off base where we pleased.

We'd go to town and come back with candy bars and little foods we could use for breakfast the next day. Things weren't looking good.

From there we went to Selfridge Field, Detroit, for our tactical training. We drove to our next assignment in my beautiful blue Chevrolet.

Some of my fellow officers and I drove the whole way; one of the officers was Chappie James, who later became a four-star general, and there was Herman Campbell and Jerome Spurlin. We had a hard time driving back against severe cold weather and 24-hour driving shifts, but we made the trip successfully but with a lot of little difficult scenarios in between.

Selfridge Field was a dream assignment. It was not far from Detroit, and Detroit was filled with beautiful colored girls.

We were flying daily, but whenever we couldn't fly, we had a ready room where we would wait for our take-off time. It would often rain, and flying was called off. We entertained our fellow troops singing or dancing. Other fellows there had beautiful voices like Hank Hervey and Virgil Daniels, the brother of the famous singer, Billy Daniels. We put our talents to good use on those rainy days.

During these times I made friends with Chappie, my tormentor from basic training. He came to Selfridge as a fighter pilot, but when the bomber division was formed, he switched. He was a big man at 6'4". He came over because there was more room in a bomber cockpit. Many others switched for the same reason.

I should have hated him forever, but we both liked entertaining and we cemented a great friendship. Men become friends under strange circumstances.

We went into Detroit frequently. There were so many Black

nightclubs. I had never seen so many in one city–clubs I had never seen the likes of: ornate, beautiful clubs with top Black entertainers–a far cry from the most sophisticated Black night clubs in San Francisco of the day. They had the best talent, too. I remember one headliner of note, Billy Eckstein, who was the greatest singer in America at that time.

I met my future wife in one of those beautiful clubs. Her name was Elsie Miller. Her good friend, Doris Ratliff married one of my bomber buddies, Fred Parker. We had a great time in Detroit.

I wasn't concerned about spending too much time at play. I was going overseas shortly, so I might as well get in as much fun as I could before I had to go to war.

Yet, while Detroit was a progressive city for Black people, it was a different story on the base.

We weren't allowed to eat in the mess hall or go into the Officer's Club. Everyone was training for combat, however, and there was very little time to talk of social differences, but we were disgruntled. The white commanding officer knew that, so a white general named O.D. Hunter came to speak to us to let us know "where our place was," in other words, to tell us to stay in our place.

He gathered the entire unit; both enlisted and commissioned men, in an auditorium on the base where we were told in no uncertain terms that we were second-class citizens.

Unit morale was low.

Our stay at Selfridge Field was cut short. The brass in

Washington decided they wanted the Black pilots out of there. The bomber pilots would be sent to Godman Field at Fort Knox, Kentucky.

Before I left, I got married on August 10, 1944. There was a bright side after all. Elsie was so beautiful, and that's what kept me going. A Reverend White married us, and Doris served as best man.

We decided to take a honeymoon. We went to Elsie's hometown of Culver, Indiana. Our best man and constant companion went with us. We drove the two hundred or so miles to Culver.

Culver is the home of a boy's military academy on beautiful Lake Maxinkuckee. We got there about midnight, surprising my Elsie's own Aunt Elsie who had raised her.

We hadn't told her we were coming or that we were married. We just drove up after midnight full of surprises.

Culver was a nice place to go for a honeymoon. I got to know and admire Elsie's uncle, Ace Byrd, and I always will admire him. Aunt Elsie and Uncle Ace worked in food service at the academy.

We visited some very pretty areas. All in all, it was a great honeymoon despite the prejudice that permeated the whole area.

Mind you, I was always in uniform, and it was wartime. I got a yearning for a milk shake. I was by myself. I stopped at a drugstore with a soda fountain on Main Street.

I sat down at the counter and the lady took my order. When she got back, the shake was in a bag to go. I said, "This is an odd way to serve a milkshake." I took it out of the bag and drank it right there at the counter.

Of course, I understood that she wanted me to take it outside, but no way a lieutenant in the air corps was going to take that. That was just one incident.

Unfortunately, we had to get back to Detroit–me to the airfield and Elsie to her job at the Office of Price Administration, where they gave out food and gas rations.

Regardless of my intimate connection with her, Elsie failed to get me any extra rations. She was a loyal employee first.

Not long after our return, I was sent to Godman Field where I lived in the Bachelor Officers Quarters, but I was on the lookout for a place in town where we could live as a married couple.

I had to arrange some way to bring Elsie to Kentucky after she completed her assignment at the O.P.A. in a few more months.

I found a place and sent for her. She came down on the train, and we made our first home at 3316 Hale Street, Louisville, Kentucky. We had a wonderful landlady named Nell McCarley, whose husband was away at war.

We stayed there at least a year. Louisville was another southern town. We went into the Black part of town to shop.

We lived in Louisville a little longer than we had expected, because in organizing the Black bomber group, we had to await the arrival of corresponding support personnel, the mechanics, fuelers, and clerks who were needed for our daily operations.

Navigators and gunners and radiomen were all undergoing their slow training process and trickled in. We never had a full set of crews to engage in combat.

In the meantime, I had an incident I know I'll never forget. I told you that I had a good deal of experience marching. I liked it from my early days of scouting. Soldiering was something I enjoyed.

It so happened that one Saturday the whole group was ordered to march on the parade grounds. However, that Saturday I was sick. I felt ill. I'm not normally sick, and I enjoyed marching so it wasn't goldbricking but I was bad off. Real sick.

I asked Major Marchbanks, the company medical officer, to be excused. It was very obvious he thought I was just trying to get out of marching. He inflicted his judgment on me, requiring me to stay alone in an empty barracks and go to bed there immediately if I was so sick.

So I did. The whole day went by, and I just lay there. Nobody came in. Nothing happened. Night fell, and I was feeling worse. I could hardly move. Fortunately, there was a Black medical doctor there – I can't remember his name – but he was an angel.

He was on duty that night as Officer of the Day. He had occasion to come to the barracks, and he saw me.

He pinched my skin, and it just clung together. I was an ugly yellow. He ordered an ambulance to take me at once to Ft. Knox Medical Center.

I was so sick I could hardly move. They had to do everything for me. I remember a doctor treating me, then I passed out.

I woke up in the morning in the hospital, and they told me I almost died. If I hadn't come in when I did, I would have died.

It turned out that I had atypical pneumonia, which shows how prejudice can alter even a doctor's diagnosis. I spent the next six weeks in that hospital. It was that bad. I never forgave Dr. Marchbanks, but I guess I do now. He's deceased.

Godman Field was like a home base. We were sent from there to several fields throughout the South for a variety of training, but we'd always go back to Godman Field before striking out on our next assignment.

I can't attest to the exact sequence of events, but somewhere along the line, our squadron, the 618th, was assigned to go to Myrtle Beach, South Carolina for live gunnery training.

Myrtle Beach was a very pretty base. Pine trees grew right down to the shore. The sand was white. Other than that, Myrtle Beach was not a pleasant assignment.

Some of us went swimming at the beach and decided to take a hike through the pines.

We reached a point where someone shouted, "Halt." There on a knoll above us was a white guy with a shotgun. He told us to get back where we came from. This was his beach. He said he didn't allow niggers on his beach.

We were only wearing bathing suits, not looking for any trouble, but did we have it. He definitely convinced us he was serious, so we went back to our beach.

That was just the beginning. I wasn't involved in any of the other trouble, so I can't exactly describe it, but the townsfolk so deeply resented our coming into town that many of the soldiers felt compelled to carry side arms on future forays for self defense. We believed it necessary to go into town in an armed group in a jeep to do our shopping. It was tense.

All throughout our tactical training, there were obvious incidents of discrimination; for example, the white officers had instructed white enlisted men not to show us proper military respect. They refused to salute us, and we'd have to "check them out" to make sure they did.

They were told—and this is a fact—that we were no better

than dogs. These enlisted men were ordered to treat us in this disrespectful manner.

One time we were flying in an area that included Georgia. On one occasion, I don't recall why, but I had need to land at the air corps base there. The custom at bases where a landing plane was not headquartered was to meet the incoming aircraft in a jeep to escort the craft to a suitable parking place on the line. Usually the jeep had a sign on the rear, "Follow Me."

A jeep came out with an officer and enlisted driver with a sign, "Follow Me," so I proceeded to follow it but couldn't as it sped away too fast to taxi after.

It didn't head toward the hangar at all but virtually disappeared. As soon as the driver saw my crew was all Black, he sped away.

Another similar occurrence was when my crew and I landed at a base in Dothan, Alabama. In this instance, there were so many planes on the line you couldn't park near the hangar so we parked at an outermost space.

In instances like this, protocol is to run an empty jeep out to the plane to ferry in the crew.

We were expecting the usual treatment. We all got out of the aircraft put our parachutes away and waited for the jeep to come.

When the driver got near to us, he saw that we were all Black. He never stopped. He just made a U-turn and headed back. We had to walk to the hangar.

Racism was everywhere. We expected it, and we usually had a little plan to counter it. We were really tested, however, when we saw German prisoners of war allowed to roam freely about our airbases while we were confined to only parts of the base. POW's were going through our barracks under the pretext of cleaning them. They could go into town but we–American soldiers willing to give up our lives in service of our country –were virtually restricted to base.

We were disheartened by the fact that some people couldn't distinguish between friend and foe. Germans flying under the banner of Hitler and Nazism were the enemy. Our fighter group was battling them overseas. The Germans were killing American soldiers and bombing their white European neighbors; they could bomb America, too.

At the same time, our government was taking Americans of Japanese descent out of their homes, taking their farms and houses and putting them into camps. There were gross inconsistencies. This policy of acting along racial lines could be putting our nation at risk. It was hard to believe these people were in their right minds. We were experiencing a very uncomfortable tension.

If we only considered how others regarded us or how others were treating us, our self-esteem would have been chipped away. But our self-respect remained intact. We could look ourselves in the eye and know we were doing our best. We wouldn't give up. We would try harder.

By the time we returned to Godman Field from Myrtle Beach, our unit had come up to full strength, having all the personnel necessary for all the flight groups. Then the order came in to move all our staff to Freeman Field that was near a town called Seymour, Indiana.

We did. Then I hitched a ride back to Louisville on one of our planes with the idea of picking Elsie up. She was pregnant, and we thought we might not have our child in Louisville but in Seymour instead.

Elsie is very fair-skinned and was seeing a white doctor in Louisville on her own for prenatal care, so when the day came to deliver, she would be taken care of by this White doctor.

We drove back to Freeman Field. We were provided married officers quarters, which were very nice, comfortable one-bedroom homes with a coal stove. They were duplex-type tract homes located near the gate to the base.

Since we most likely wouldn't have the baby in Louisville, we thought one of these Indiana towns would do. We were in a kind of hilly, rural section of the state. We found a doctor in a town called Brownsville. He seemed to be considerate and compassionate, and he became our anticipated obstetrician.

But Seymour and Freeman Field turned out to be very unfriendly places, too. The soldiers' and officers' wives stopped shopping in town because the townspeople made it very clear we wouldn't be served. It was another tense, testy situation.

We were able to live on the base with little trouble as a family. As far as military life and the white officers were concerned though, our treatment was severely humiliating.

Freeman was designated a Black training field on the spot. All the white troops had to leave, but the white officers stayed. They were definitely in the minority, something like twenty to one Black to White officers.

The local townspeople served as barbers, clerks, and the like. When Freeman changed to a colored field, the white people were given the choice of remaining or leaving. Many chose to stay because work must have been hard to come by in that small, isolated place.

About the most prominent memory I have of the civilian employees was the difficulty that the barbers had learning to cut Black people's hair. They adjusted, and everything worked out pretty well.

The few White officers held all the top command positions. Many of the young White officers had less military experience than we did. Still, with less flying experience, they were there to train us. It was a joke to us.

I'm sure it was an undesirable stint in their training, but it was beneficial nevertheless. They would, of course, be promoted from lieutenant to captain then they would leave. A stint with us meant an automatic promotion for them.

They were taking the ranks we were supposed to have so we remained 2nd lieutenants for the longest time. It became very difficult to serve enthusiastically under those conditions.

There was a very nice officers club at Freeman, very posh inside. We weren't allowed to use it. We were given an empty barracks with a ping-pong table to use as our officers club. We weren't allowed to use many of the base facilities. We were told we couldn't assemble in groups of greater than three, that we couldn't use certain buildings or even cross certain fields. The buildings were reserved for the "trainers'. The fields were designated as recreation areas for the "trainers." "Trainers" was the distinction they used to cover up racial segregation.

This was written as an order, and we were told to sign it. Some of us did, some of us didn't. We couldn't think of anything we'd done to warrant this written proclamation. I still have a copy of it.

We resented this as we were training for combat using live ammunition. We knew the next stop was combat overseas. We didn't want to go overseas into combat with this discrimination going on.

We had many discussions about our mistreatment. We made statements directly to the White officers that we had many more hours flying time than they had and much more experience.

There was always that hostility. We would always talk about how we were going to handle this situation, what we were going to do, but underneath it all, there was a war going on and we were very patriotic.

Regardless of the racism going on, we wanted to get overseas and try out our skills because we felt we were the best pilots in the whole doggone air corps.

When the inexperienced White "trainers" took us up and into our maneuvers, we would strive to excel, flying our best in formation–you name it, we did it.

Despite the constant tension, we were all together in this, and we didn't slacken a bit in our training. We were brothers. We didn't say, "Let's take this and not complain…" Nor did any of us become radical pushing for more overt action. We were just all in it together. We did everything in a conscientious way. We discussed thoroughly issues like practicality and repercussions, and we became very close.

11

Double V Campaign

Eventually, we decided to go to the officers club but in a haphazard way. One or two of us would drift into the club and ask for drinks, but we were denied. Next, we got together to devise a plan to protest this treatment in a proper military manner. We had meetings in the mess hall at night, examining our situation with all the intensity of scientists looking through their microscopes or observing the movement of the planets.

We found nothing redeeming about the situation except that the white officers perhaps provided an aura of legitimacy to our operations to the powers-that-be. We were indignant. Did they think we couldn't tell the difference between officer's accommodations and a card table and folding chairs?

Were these men qualified to train us? Or was the intent to bombard us with insults to erode our confidence and cause the project to fail? This policy of giving promotions based upon skin color was nothing to be proud of. These policies were not democracy as we understood it.

We had to figure out a strategy to bring our mistreatment to light. We wanted to make sure we were clearly being excluded from use of the club, so we decided to send groups of three officers at a time to demand service and see if we would be served.

I went over to the club with two other officers, Hank Hervey and 'Hatch' Hunter. Sure enough, when we sat down at the bar and ordered a drink, the bartender said, "You can't be served here."

I looked around, and there were some white officers at tables in the back of the bar with their backs to us. You could see their necks getting redder and redder with anger or embarrassment as they sat in stony insularity. Surely they knew of our exploits overseas even if they didn't care to know about our lives and our accomplishments prior to our arrival at Tuskegee.

I said, "Look, we all fly here together. We all work here together. Why can't we relax together?"

The bartender had nothing more to say, of course. We didn't create any problems. We just walked away.

Then other groups of three would go in and be refused. We got our clear refusal. We were not to use that club.

One of the groups of three included an officer named Roger Terry. They went to the officer's club and were met at the door by the officer in charge of the bar, some white major, and they were told to leave. In the process of leaving, Terry brushed against the white major.

The white officer would eventually file charges of assaulting an officer against all three men.

In the meantime, about three hundred of us–pilots, officers, navigators–decided one afternoon that those who didn't have flight duties that day would put on their uniforms and march on the officer's club. We thought that with so many of us, they couldn't refuse us all.

About one hundred of us formed a parade. We marched right down to the officer's club, intending to go in. However, when we got there, the white major in charge of the club was standing in front of the door, smoking a pipe, and there was a big padlock on the door.

He says, "You gotta be fast. The officer's club is closed."

When he said that, it was clear to us that somebody told him what we were doing.

But it drew attention to our dispute. The very next day, a stormy day, so bad even the birds didn't want to fly, they arrested fifty single officers and fifty married officers. They did this arbitrarily. They didn't care who they were.

Without any chance to settle their affairs, they took the men to the flight line, lined them all up and put them on cargo planes bound for Godman Field. At Godman Field they were quartered in a stockade surrounded by concertina wire and floodlights. They kept 101 officers as prisoners charged with mutiny. They had characterized our actions as a mutiny.

What they hadn't thought about was the Black press. The *Pittsburgh Courier* had been running a Double V campaign under the theme, "Democracy: Victory at Home, Victory Abroad." Black soldiers were serving willingly in the armed forces. If we were expected to give our lives overseas, we should expect full citizenship at home.

When we formed our action, we had called the Black press. *The Pittsburgh Courier, The Chicago Defender, The Afro-American* and New York's *Amsterdam News* sent reporters down to the field.

We put them up in a little housing area just off base because they weren't permitted on the field. They would get the stories as we came off base for the day.

The day they arrested and flew all those men out, the press got the story and wired it all over the country. The article said that there was a mutiny, and 101 officers were arrested. There was also a picture.

A reporter had given an enlisted man a belt camera to get a picture of the line up. He went down to the flight line and opened his overcoat so that the belt buckle with the camera had a clear shot. He took pictures of the men lined up in front of the airplanes.

When the pictures ran in the newspapers, a public outcry was created. The War Department became very nervous about arresting these officers, who by this time had become an elite group able to voice our grievances. How could the United States explain to the enemy that we had this internal dispute, but they subsequently held a court-martial for everyone.

All but three of the arrested officers were eventually released and exonerated. One of the three remaining, Roger Terry, was made the scapegoat convicted of assaulting an officer and dishonorably discharged. They let the other two go.

The occasion created such a stir in Washington and elsewhere that the white commander, Col. Selway, who was accused of being the source of the problem, was relieved of his command. All the white officers were replaced. The rest of the base was ordered closed and all the personnel there were ordered back to Godman.

They brought in General Benjamin O. Davis, Jr. from overseas, where he had been the head of the Red Tail fighter pilots in North Africa and Italy. Under Davis' command our segregated fighter groups had destroyed or hit over 409 German airplanes, 950 ground units, and sunk a battleship destroyer from the air with machine gun fire.

Our ground crew commandeered a German supply train for equipment to retrofit our planes and make them ready for the missions we were assigned; otherwise, they may have been suicide missions.

The timing was perfect as Davis was due to rotate back to the States, and all the Black officers who had served so meritoriously under him would assume the training at Tuskegee. We finally became an all-Black unit, but they called our incident the "Freeman Field Mutiny."

I was assigned to fly one of the B25's back to Godman, so I was unable to drive Elsie there. My friend Hank Hervey drove Elsie back in my car.

It was raining and lightning. We heard of flooding in the surrounding parts of the state en route to Godman Field. They ran into flooded bridges on the road, had to take many detours, but finally made it to Louisville.

We set up housekeeping again. Elsie went back to the doctor she'd been going to previously. It was at this time we were sent to Myrtle Beach for gunnery.

While I was at Myrtle Beach, Elsie went into labor. She's in

Kentucky, and I'm in South Carolina. Hank's wife took her to the hospital and there they waited for Elsie's doctor.

When he got there and saw Hank's wife, who was obviously colored, he refused to deliver Elsie. She was in labor and in a terrible predicament. She had been afraid all along that if she had a brown baby in a white hospital they might take the baby away from her or commit some other horrific act.

The private room she had arranged was no longer available to her. She was placed in a room alone in the Black section of the hospital. This may have been the safest move for the delivery after all.

I tried, but I couldn't get back in time for the birth. They allowed me leave but I had to hitchhike taking the first available plane. By the time I arrived Penny was born. Our dream of having our daughter in Brownsville was shattered, but we were still excited about our first child.

Elsie and I got back into the habit of living as man and wife in Louisville. Penny kept growing. Our outfit swelled in number, and rumor had it, we were to be moved to the South Pacific to do our part in the war.

It seemed obvious we'd be going to the South Pacific because they would have us practice ditching our planes over a mock ocean and seeing how quickly we could evacuate the plane.

It was obvious we weren't going to Europe where the fighter contingent was setting remarkable records. In the meantime, we kind of settled down because those rumors about the South Pacific never materialized.

Racial incidents happened in Louisville often. To say that we couldn't go to this restaurant or buy these items was no news as that was customary in Louisville.

But one time, Hank Hervey and I decided to go to the ballpark. Louisville had a beautiful ballpark, and the park had been taken over by Blacks for an all-colored Negro League ball game. We definitely wanted to see them.

Hank and I got seats right down behind home plate. At least, we bought tickets for that area.

We were shocked to find out we couldn't sit in those seats for an all-colored baseball game.

When we tried to get to our seats, a couple of white men stopped us and asked where we were going. We showed them our tickets and got into a little verbal exchange.

It's amazing how quickly a mob formed. Before we knew it, we were talking to more than just two white men. We were talking to a mob. They made no bones about it, that if we didn't go away something serious would happen to us.

That was the height of absurdity. You couldn't go to an all-colored contest at a time when the white team wasn't using the field.

These behaviors didn't make sense to Marion Anderson either. Marion Anderson was world-renowned: the first African-American operatic singer to become a permanent member of the Metropolitan Opera Company.

She was on tour and was scheduled to perform in Louisville, but she cancelled when she learned the theater she was to perform in wouldn't allow coloreds.

After the turnover when Davis returned, however, things were harmonious in our all Black outfit. Davis was a peerless leader.

He graduated from the U.S. Military Academy at West Point, New York, in 1936. He was only the fourth African American ever to do so.

He had been shunned at the academy. Other cadets refused to speak with him except for official reasons. He had no roommate in the dormitory and no one else assigned to his tent in the field. He ate his meals without a word for four years and still made it through. There was no one better the Tuskegee forces could serve under.

We eventually ended up at Lockbourn Air Force Base near Columbus, Ohio. The Black Air Corps stayed there several years.

Elsie and I moved with the other families and found a nice rental in Columbus. Shortly after arrival, we decided to buy our first home. There were some small, well-built brick homes in Columbus that were selling at a very reasonable price.

I recall our payments were $45.00 a month. We bought a brick home, improved it, furnished it to a small degree, and enjoyed living there very much. We were neighbors to another bomber pilot, Charles Walker, and we had a great little community there.

We weren't in Columbus long when they sent us out to California to Blythe, one of the hottest places on earth, near Death Valley.

Our mission was to do over-water flying. Many of our missions took us out over the Pacific Ocean where we would bomb islands for practice.

Blythe was a place no one would wish on a spouse, so no one

brought their wives, and it was just as well for Blythe was a very prejudiced little town. Not necessarily to Blacks, but it was signs like, "No dogs or Indians allowed," that gave us the idea that racism against Blacks was easily found in Blythe. We didn't do too much shopping there.

It was a welcome day when we received orders back to Lockbourn. I was in charge of a 6-plane flight for the return journey, and we made it back in record time. Not long after that, the war ended.

The bomb was dropped on Hiroshima, and Japan surrendered soon after. Shortly after that, we became a peacetime air corps.

Some flying officers were reduced to non-flying status. I was stationed briefly at Selma, Alabama. William "Chubby" Green and myself were assigned to Selma Army Air Corps Base for administrative training. We were the only two Black people in our class of about a thousand.

Selma would become famous for the march to Montgomery over the Edmund Pettus Bridge with Dr. Martin Luther King, Jr. I traveled that bridge almost every day. I had a modern, streamlined Packard—not your usual car. The model was called Zephyr, I believe. When we went into town, we would drive my Zephyr.

Every time we drove into town we had an escort. The police would tail us immediately upon entering town and follow us everywhere. They did this every time we went to town, so you might guess that my driving was impeccable. And the places we went had to be acceptable to our rear-escort as well. That was an uncomfortable feeling but my driving was appropriate for the situation.

My memory of Selma is of a desolate little town. The colored folks had their own neighborhood. You had no trouble telling which neighborhood you were in, just look at the street. If it was paved, you weren't in the colored quarter. That neighborhood had muddy dirt streets, while the rest of town was paved.

Things were kind of humdrum and going at a slow pace after the war. The War Department was planning how to discharge surplus troops.

In our case, we could remain in the service with a minimum three-year re-enlistment, or we could get out right away.

This was 1947, and Elsie and I opted out of the service to take our chances in civilian life. We quit the service and headed back for California in our car with all of our belongings and our precious Penny, now two years old. We sold the house in Columbus and put the money away for future use.

The ride back was uneventful. You can bet that we had lots of difficulty on the way, getting lodging, getting meals, getting gas—just about everything. We were anxious to get back to California where we thought we could escape racism.

12

Victory at Home

I kept telling Elsie on the trip back, "Just wait till we get to California. Then we can get rid of all this prejudice and start living like human beings."

We crossed the border into California, down near the tip of Arizona, passing through Blythe. It was about noontime and we thought we'd get a hamburger.

I stopped at a likely looking spot. It did sell hamburgers. I had this big, sleek, streamlined silver gray Packard that I parked in front, leaving Elsie and Penny behind in the car.

I went inside. The place had a counter and a dining room. I sat at the counter because I wanted take-out.

I looked around and noticed a man in the dining room section going from table to table saying something to the diners and pointing his finger at me. He did this to everyone in the dining room.

Some people left. I looked outside and saw a group forming.

Finally this guy came up to an empty stool on my right and sat down. He just sat there. I asked, "What's the matter?"

He said, "Just wait until you leave and you'll find out."

I became uneasy, started sweating and looking around for a weapon to defend myself should there be a fight. All I could see was the salt and pepper shakers in front of me, so I put a shaker in each hand while he sat there waiting.

Finally, I spun around on my stool to face him and asked again, "Look, what's the matter?"

When I spun around, he saw my pilot wings on my left breast. He immediately said, "Oh, he's an air corps officer. That's different."

"What's different," I asked.

And he said, "Well, I just got out of the service, and I promised myself that the first officer I see, I'm going to beat him up."

I relaxed all of a sudden because it wasn't racial. It was a rank thing.

By that time, a big crowd had gathered outside. There was no one left in the dining room. My hamburgers came, and I had to leave. I opened the screen door and started to walk, but the crowd hemmed me in. I knew I had to walk through that crowd. The car wasn't far away, but it seemed miles through that crowd.

I heard voices saying, "Get that nigger! Get him! You gonna let him get away?"

I bit my lip and started walking. Miraculously, I shouldered my way through a narrow path they finally allowed me. I got to the car where Elsie and little Penny were waiting, and although I needed some gas and the nearest station was a mile down the road, we took off as fast as we could, leaving that terrible experience behind.

We finally got to San Mateo, to 114 S. Delaware Street, where our family had lived for decades. The sense of relief we all felt was palpable.

My mother, as a surprise, had built a two-bedroom apartment for us at the rear of the house.

13

Victory at Home II

Since I didn't need to find a place for my family to live, I focused on getting a job. I felt certain I could go back to teaching dance classes, but with my five years experience as a bomber pilot I felt I might qualify as a commercial airline pilot, but I was wrong.

The San Francisco airport, called Mills Field at that time, was just one big room with counters for each of the airlines flying out of there.

One day, I went to Mills Field with all my pilots' credentials the FAA had given us before we left the service, including a commercial license. They were called multi-engine land licenses that are good for a lifetime.

I noticed that white flight veterans were going for jobs with the airlines, so I went in and asked at the first airline I came to if they would hire me as a pilot. They almost laughed in my face. I went to the next one and told them I was seeking a job as a commercial pilot, could I fly for them? This fellow was audacious enough to say, "You could fly that broom over in the corner."

I went to about four more airlines and got the same reaction everywhere. It was disheartening. I was simply trying to live a regular life as a citizen of the United States and a regular human being but everything around me was changing. The population was growing as many defense workers decided to stay in the Bay Area after the war. Even the geography was changing with dredging of the bay and marshes filled in and highways cut through wilderness.

I asked myself what resources did I have? I needed to take care of my family. I could open up a dance studio based on my reputation before the war or, the other option was that I could go to school. I already had two years of college.

I had my mind dead-set on going to Stanford. I drove up the palm-lined entrance to campus and enrolled as a veteran with no trouble. I would have never been able to afford tuition without the G.I. Bill, so returning to school wasn't going to be too much of a financial burden.

The government bought all my books, paid tuition, and provided me with a stipend. I still had to work to supplement those funds because they weren't quite enough to maintain my growing family.

I discovered the campus had only two Blacks when I attended, both of us veterans of the war. Our acceptance was more than likely based on the fact we were veterans, also Californians, and our grades were acceptable.

We weren't the first Black people to attend Stanford. Frank Collier, whom I grew up with in San Mateo, graduated in 1941 before the war.

I came across some books listing all Stanford graduates throughout its history since its founding in 1891. In those days, when a colored person was referred to in publications or documents at Stanford, he or she was designated as such with either 'colored' or with an asterisk following his or her name and a footnote. They were always careful to separate Negroes from the rest of the student body.

I learned there were six Black students before us. The first was in the very first graduating class. I believe he was from Augusta, Georgia. At that time, there were no Black athletes on any of the teams –none. In fact, the year I graduated was the first year they had a Black basketball player named Eddie Tucker.

I was 28 years old when I arrived at Stanford in 1947. I felt like an old man amongst my younger classmates and because I'd been through the racial cauldron in the air corps, I was very alert to racism wherever it reared its ugly head. And it did, often.

I found myself at odds with a history teacher, for example, who referred to Blacks in a consistently derogatory manner in the classroom. Professor Bailey stated that, "All Negroes are ignorant, lazy, and speak in a crude manner and had to be tolerated by the population at-large."

I had many conversations with him privately where I disputed his theory and pointed out the accomplishments of Negroes in all walks of life: accomplishments in statesmanship, theatre, and medicine–in just about every field of endeavor you care to mention. Negroes also developed numerous important inventions.

Fortunately, he listened, and I think I converted at least one man to being at least curious about Negro contributions and giving credit where credit is due. After a few sessions in his office, he changed his opinion and didn't agree to like Black people, but he did alter the negative tone towards Blacks in his lectures.

I also had trouble with a phonetics professor who claimed all Blacks had the same accent and "talked lahk thiyas" with a Southern accent. I had to point out to him that while in the service I met Black people from all over the United States, and each had an accent characteristic of his respective locale just like Whites in the United States.

The professor had difficulty believing that and gave me a poor grade, maybe a C or worse, but I couldn't sit quietly in his classroom and let him promulgate those myths when I had seen with my own eyes men and women who proved on a fundamental level the fallacy of his beliefs.

Needless to say, I was sensitive when I was at Stanford and still can't feel any deep sense of commitment to the university. I couldn't feel any school spirit, camaraderie, or hail-fellows-well-met because when my classes ended each day I had to hustle back to San Mateo to teach dancing.

If I had known that Truman would issue Executive Order 9981 in 1948 mandating desegregation of the military, I may have stayed in the air corps because I was encountering nothing but problems.

When I wanted to rent a place for my dance studio, I had to apply to the San Mateo city fathers for permission to use an old house in a neighborhood slowly becoming semi-commercial from its former residential status.

I had to go through a process that found me at one point in front of the city planners. The public was allowed to attend the meetings.

The city planners turned me down. They denied my application.

Based on my experience up to this point, it would have been very easy for me to hate all white people but when I was fighting the planning commission and the council just to get an application to go into business, I got an anonymous phone call from a white man who said if I was able to get my permit, he'd loan me $500 to do so.

I got the permit, and he called me and left his phone number. I can't recall his name, but he gave me a $500.00 loan, no interest and no specified time to pay it back. I'm glad I ran into that man. He helped me stay open to the possibility that not all white people are prejudiced.

Despite battling the planning commission and teaching dance, I graduated from Stanford in 1949. I brought my mother, my wife, and daughters to the graduation ceremonies, hoping this wouldn't be my last drive up the nearly mile long roadway to campus.

Prior to graduation, I had applied to Stanford's law school. At that time there had been no colored students in the law school ever. I learned later that the first colored applicant to Stanford Law School didn't graduate until 1969.

I imagine that my attempt to get into law school there might have been a futile attempt. I did harbor thoughts at that time that I was being blocked from admission by the authorities there. At that time, the law school exam was not uniform, and there were exams that differed from others.

I believe I received one of those hard ones. Even if I had been Oliver Wendell Holmes, I believe I couldn't have passed the exam, and I was right. I didn't. So I put my education on hold and went back to teaching dance full time.

My studio flourished as I developed a nice-sized following. Three years after I rented the house, I could foresee buying property and building my own dance studio.

I had enough money saved to buy a vacant lot a block down from the building I was renting and I sought a building permit from the city council.

The lot sat a block down the street on San Mateo Drive. I felt I could be successful on this street–it was the same street that ran next to my father's building.

I sought financing from a local bank and was approved for the loan. The loan officer told me not to come back. I don't know of he was trying to tell me something or if he was generally ill mannered.

I bought the lot for $10,000 that I paid over three years. I was ready to build. I learned I had to get a building permit and seek approval again from the planning commission and city council.

The planning commission denied my permit. I had to have a public hearing, and they made it official by denying me at the hearing.

I still had one more chance, and that was to pass the council's scrutiny. The council was made up of seven people. One of them, the mayor, was a fellow my brother went through school with who was a good friend.

I didn't hire a lawyer. I represented myself, but I also had the very able assistance of a real estate broker. When it came time for the council to vote, it was deadlocked three to three.

In cases of a deadlock the mayor casts the deciding vote. He cast his vote in favor of granting the permit. When they announced it in the public hall, the place went into an uproar. Women threw their purses at me. For me, it became a big, noisy celebration. We were dancing in the street.

By now we had two children. My second daughter, Paula Michelle, was born at Mills Hospital in San Mateo. I had always wanted San Mateo to be the place my children were born.

I moved out of my mother's house as it was getting a little crowded after my brother Barney and his wife moved in, too. To maintain harmony and get some space, I rented a home away from my mother but still in San Mateo

While Elsie and I were saving up to build our studio on our lot, ironically an opportunity arose to move into Hillsborough, a very exclusive area that at the time certainly had no colored property owners.

A fellow named Henry Fonda (not the actor) called us up to ask if we'd like to buy his house. I was curious, so we went over to see his house located on the fringe of Hillsborough near Burlingame.

The house was very nice. We asked him about the terms on the mortgage. He made the deal sound interesting, but the house had some shortcomings.

No less than a quarter acre parcel, the house was small with only two bedrooms and one bath. That didn't appeal to us as we already had two children and we needed more than two bedrooms and certainly more than one bath.

I remember he took us out into the yard, turned the radio up full blast while he was talking, explaining that he didn't want the neighbors to hear our conversation, which I later understood. But we decided to concentrate on building the dance studio.

Since I wasn't able to enter law school, I decided to exert all my energy making my dancing business thrive. I needed to increase business as Elsie and I adopted Patrick, one of Elsie's sister's sons. Now we had a third child in our family.

Life became somewhat routine. I worked at the studio. My children attended school, and Elsie helped at the studio as receptionist, secretary, and Jill of all trades designing costumes and stage sets. We settled into a comfortable lifestyle.

I had started an annual dance recital that became a very popular local event and increased attendance at my studio. Some recitals were performed for charities, and I think I improved my image as a businessman in the community.

Soon it became possible to think about buying a home of our own. We had been living in small homes with our family of five.

We found a huge lot on top of a hill where we could see forever. This was in the town of Belmont, immediately south of

San Mateo. I believe that at the time there were no Black people living there.

We called the owner, a Welshman, and I gave my name as Williams and he presumed I was Welsh, too, as Williams is a common Welsh name. When I eventually met him in person, he was clearly disappointed. Still, he went ahead with our deal.

When word got out that a colored person had bought this lot, I started receiving anonymous phone calls threatening that, "If you ever start to build, we'll never let you finish. We'll break out all your windows and cut up your beams."

I discovered that one of the callers was a local real estate agent named Rupert Taylor who carried a lot of influence with the Belmont city council, so he was a formidable foe.

I suggested to him that he buy me out, which he did instantly leaving me wishing I had asked for much more money, but I turned a tidy profit and put most of the money back into the dance studio.

Life settled back into a normal pace with Elsie and me running the studio, our children off at local schools for the day. We took some of our real estate profits and bought another lot in Belmont a little lower on the hill.

To do so, we had to have a white friend make the purchase for us, as it appeared lots were not available to colored people in Belmont.

After a petition drive was attempted to bar us from building, the City of Belmont held a council meeting. After much discussion, one man, Del Woodin, stood up to say that he'd rather live next to us than anyone else at the meeting.

The lot was located across the street from a large chrysanthemum nursery with acres of fragrant flowers. It was rumored the nursery was to be sold to make way for single-family upper-scale homes, but that all changed.

Rupert Taylor came back into the picture. The Belmont city council was manipulated into rezoning the area for apartment buildings instead. Apartments were built, and they rise all around our home today.

The lot we had was a corner lot. Our house was built to face the chrysanthemum nursery and future single-family houses, but apartments loom in front of our home today. They're like a wall on the hill above us blocking any view to the west thus lowering the value of our home.

When our house was completed, we moved in without incident in 1956. After living there a short while, our neighbors to the east added a fence to our side and painted it black, perhaps a reflection of their feelings towards us. Eventually they moved away.

Another time, someone placed a noose in a tree in front of the house. When I told a colleague in the performing arts about the incident and how my wife and children were alone in the house at the time, he offered to sit outside our house with a rifle, but after that, there was no further overt harassment.

I reached a level of respect in the community. I was invited to join the Kiwanis Club of San Mateo. I believe I was the first colored member on the peninsula.

In 1965, they made me president of Kiwanis, and that gave me a feeling of pride because they were a decent group of men and they accorded me all the respect a president should get.

One of the interesting moments I had as president was to

host and sit with Shirley Temple Black, long past the child actor but still a thrill to talk with and reminisce a bit about her past, particularly the films she made with Bill 'Bo Jangles' Robinson.

The dance studio was thriving and I became a part of several dance organizations and president of the National Association of Dance and Affiliated Artists.

The most interesting time I had as a dancer was being selected by Dance Caravan to teach summer courses on the latest trends to dancers and dance teachers all over the United States. I taught the latest trends in tap.

This was at a time when race relations between Blacks and Whites were very tense. Rosa Parks had refused to give up her seat on a bus in Alabama, and a boycott began with Martin Luther King, Jr., bringing hope to Black people. White sheriffs were unleashing ferocious dogs on civil rights marchers and blasting them with fire hoses.

At this time, Black people were protesting separation and exclusion from public facilities and restaurants. It was a time when Black people were sending their children to White schools under the protection of the National Guard, when freedom riders, both black and white, were murdered trying to secure the right to vote for Black people.

My boss, who had hired me to travel with this dance caravan, was aware of the tensions. He was a friend of mine from San Francisco. He told me I didn't have to make the first stop in South Carolina, so I joined up at the second stop instead, finishing the remaining nine stops and ending up in New York.

There were several incidents of small consequence along the way. I was the first Black dance instructor on the tour, a fact of which I was aware, and that kept me on my guard.

In Birmingham, Alabama, I spent three days teaching the latest tap trends. At the end of the stay, as we all were assembled in the lobby of our hotel, one of the teachers came up to me and said with a smile on her face, "See, we don't treat niggers so bad, do we?"

I was also being a good Kiwanian while on tour, seeking out the local Kiwanis meetings to fill up some time.

Every once in a while I would find a meeting. This was in the 60's, and I didn't realize how deep racism was still so when I attempted to go to a meeting in Atlanta, Georgia, the attendance secretary got nervous and said, "No, you don't have to attend the meeting. I'll give you your attendance slip. You don't need to go in there." I took my slip and moved on.

The next time, I had a plan. A famous speaker was drawing quite a crowd. I decided that rather than trying to impose myself on someone and ask to join their table, I would arrive early and seat myself at an empty table, forcing those who arrived late to sit around me.

I arrived early and sat at a table. All the other tables around me filled up. No one sat at my table. People were standing around my table–all these fellow Kiwanis. But that didn't bother me.

Finally, reluctantly, people sat at the table, and it filled up. Nobody spoke to me, of course, but at least I got to hear a great speaker.

I still was flying. I joined a private flying club, but I was interested in the Air Force Reserves. If I stayed active in the reserves I earned flight hours toward a small pension, and I got to fly.

The nearest place for reserve duty was Hamilton Field, nearly an hour's drive from San Mateo. I went to sign up, but there were too many applicants which meant I would get little, if any, flying time.

No flying time and the possibility of having to serve in active status if war broke out added up to leaving the Air Force Reserves. Sure enough, the Korean War broke out in 1950 and some of my reserve friends went to war.

The 1960's were quiet years at home. My business was successful, and I continued to do annual recitals and shows for charity. I enjoyed a clientele of top Peninsula families as well as every other income strata. But I wasn't content. Something was missing. I felt I should continue my education and become something more than just a dance teacher.

Sure, everyone knows colored folks can dance, but I thought I had abilities that surpassed the dance floor. I decided to go to law school. I wanted to be a lawyer.

Up until the '60's, Stanford Law School had never had a Black student. The first to graduate did so in the '60's. I wanted to go to Stanford Law School and Stanford only. My desire to become a lawyer centered on that. I had no desire to go to law school anywhere else.

Since I lived in close proximity to Stanford, I could live at home and attend classes. With a short commute, I could teach dance classes in the evening.

I ran into problems getting into school. An early attempt to get in through normal channels failed, but along the way, I met a graduate, a man about my age who knew the dean of the Law School personally, and he arranged a meeting between the dean and myself.

I'm pretty sure the dean wasn't impressed with a fifty-year-old Black man, and I wasn't sure my undergraduate grades compared with my potential peers. However, by that time, Stanford had instituted a program to attract Black students. Perhaps six were enrolled. A Black lawyer named Thelton Henderson, a distinguished attorney of the civil rights era, was head of the program for minorities and the dean introduced me to him.

If it wasn't for Thelton Henderson, I don't think I would have become a Stanford lawyer. He was one very nice person, very helpful, and he got me in. This was 1970.

Surprisingly, I wasn't the oldest member in my class. One person was about six months older than me, though I don't think we had similar backgrounds. He was white and had been an employee of Stanford for about thirty years in the book-publishing department. He had constantly studied Stanford publications as part of his job.

I had no real preparation for law school, which became apparent the first day. We were assigned a hundred pages of reading prior to the first day of class, before even knowing whom our instructor would be.

A white law student was assigned to help the minority students. One of the keys for success is to become part of a study group. Because I was older than some of the professors, the younger students didn't naturally gravitate toward me. I ended up in no study group at all. To compensate, a young law school graduate helped me on my way.

I really needed him, and I owe him a sincere debt of gratitude. I only remember his name was Ted.

Stanford Law School was one of the most arduous experiences I had in my life, including the Air Corps. I was overwhelmed with the study load and by the requirement to learn the lexicon and "think as a lawyer." No one in my family had been a lawyer so this was my first exposure.

I just had a miserable time throughout. I would be getting up at 3 or 4 in the morning to study as I felt I had to have absolute quiet. I abandoned the dance studio. It was impossible for me to do anything other than attend classes and study.

In fact, I sold the studio for what I thought was a handsome price, but I was mistaken as a housing boom occurred within a month or so and similar properties were selling for up to four times as much. At the time, I was grateful for the price I got, as things for us were slim.

I felt about law school similarly to how I felt as an air corps cadet: the fear of washing out, the end of a career possible at any moment.

I always worried whether I could maintain a level footing. I constantly feared failing. But at the end of my first year, they told me I could go on to the second year and, until I realized what I was in for, I was temporarily filled with pride and confidence.

Several students, including a black student, were dismissed after their first year, but here I was going into another year.

I might mention that law school for everyone else was normally a three-year course of study. For we minority students the course was set for four years, so we didn't have to carry such a heavy course load. This wasn't as beneficial as it sounds.

Many of the subjects are interrelated. Stretching out our course work served only to remove this aspect from our experience and make learning more difficult.

I completed the third year. Another black student was dismissed but I was still there. So I was entering my fourth year, my senior year and I felt happy and triumphant to be still a part of the process.

I graduated. I don't know my exact academic ranking within my class, whether I was in the top ten or the bottom ten, but I didn't care. I got the very same diploma, and that was my goal. It's one of those things they can't take away from you. Now I'll always be a Stanford lawyer.

I didn't know then that my troubles were just beginning. Not only do you have to have a law degree, you have to have a business license to practice law in whatever state you work. I had to take the California Bar Exam. It took as long for me to pass the exam as it took to finish law school.

I never lost my determination to become a practicing California lawyer, but to be a lawyer of any kind I went to Florida and passed their bar exam first.

Florida didn't require residency, and although some complained how hard the exam was, I passed the first time. With a license I could get a job with the federal government and study to pass the California exam at a later time.

I also took the bar exam in Indiana. Even if I didn't get government work, my wife was from Indiana and we thought perhaps we could get legal work in her old home state.

I passed that exam the first time also with no trouble. So I had a Florida license, an Indiana license, but no California license. I would try to get work with a federal agency.

I applied to numerous agencies with no success. There was an opportunity to work for the National Endowment for the Arts, which I would have liked because of my experience in the entertainment field. The job required moving to Washington, D.C., however, and I didn't want to do that.

I never became a federal lawyer, and I kept trying to bust that California bar exam until I finally won.

I taught dance at Stanford for a brief while. During this time Black people were affirming their identity through the Civil Rights and the Black Power movements. We started bringing attention to our contributions to America such as Charles Drew's discovery of blood plasma, the invention of the stoplight, clothes dryer, and numerous other contributions.

Since my background was in dance, I developed a lecture on the contribution of Black people to American dance. I interviewed notables like musician Eubie Blake, who composed songs such as "Memories of You" and "I'm Just Wild About Harry", Honey Coles, former manager of the Apollo Theater, the Nicholas Brothers, Katherine Dunham, and many others.

I saw American dance as a blending of cultural forms–Irish clog dancing with arms held down tightly against the torso blended with African rhythms in tap and movement of the torso incorporated into American dance by Ms. Dunham.

I thought that the leadership of Martin Luther King, Jr. and the research of African American scholars would bring about recognition of our invaluable service to America's development, but this is still a work in progress.

Nevertheless, I introduced my children to artists no matter what their color–from Paul Robeson to Rudolph Nureyev, from Maria Tallchief to Pearl Primus.

In order to exist I also tried the real estate field, not very successfully, but it kept food on the table and my kids in school through college.

14

Legacy

Penny earned two degrees from Stanford, and Paula earned a BA from Chico State and her MA from Mills College. They both taught at an historically Black college (HBCU) in Texas–Prairie View A&M University, part of the Texas A&M University System. Penny agreed to teach there to share her Stanford education with African American youth.

Unlike California, Texas established parallel institutions for Blacks and Whites. When Texas A&M was built, Prairie View was built at the same time. Blacks in Texas would have more opportunity than Blacks in California to enter the professions. For example, Prairie View graduates more engineering students than any other university in the country. Similarly, Tuskegee Institute, another HBCU in Alabama, gave me the opportunity to fly.

My horizons were clearly expanded at Tuskegee by meeting so many accomplished men and women eager to serve their country.

I became aware of possibilities other than cooking or entertaining that were among the few opportunities California had to offer.

The Tuskegee Airmen hold an annual national convention to honor the bonds we formed during our experience in World War II. We meet on a regular basis with our local chapters throughout the year to promote flying and sponsor flying school for disadvantaged youth.

During the course of that experiment at Tuskegee to see if Black men were capable of flying and of being responsible, we flew over 15,500 sorties and more than 1,578 missions. We earned 150 Distinguished Flying Crosses, Legions of Merit, eight Purple Hearts, and the Red Star of Yugoslavia.

B.O. Davis became the first Black general in the U.S. Air Force. Daniel "Chappie" James became our nation's first Black Four-Star General, and Lucius Theus achieved the rank of Major General.

As for Roger Terry and the 101 men of the 477th Medium Bombardment Group arrested at Freeman Field, after some fifty years had passed, in 1995, Assistant Secretary of the Air Force Rodney Coleman announced that the Air Force would exonerate all of the officers involved in the Freeman Field incident.

Sixty years later on March 29. 2007, the Tuskegee Airmen were honored with the Congressional Gold Medal, the highest civilian award bestowed by the United States Congress. Only a few hundred of the original group was alive to receive recognition for their accomplishments.

This included pilots and ground crew, who also performed outstandingly to keep the pilots in the air and to operate a fully functioning segregated unit of the Army Air Corps.

We all convened in Washington, D.C. in the U.S. Capitol

rotunda. As authorized under the law, the president presented the specially designed Gold Medal on behalf of Congress.

We were of course deeply appreciative of the award, but many felt it was a long-time coming.

In 2007 when the City of Belmont found out they had a Tuskegee Airman living in their city, I was given the key to the city. Ironically, this is the same city that had to hold a council meeting in the 1950's to decide whether my family would be able to live there.

In the meantime, I participated in civil rights marches in my hometown of San Mateo to support Dr. Martin Luther King, Jr. who was struggling to awaken the consciousness of American democracy. He said:

I am cognizant of the interrelatedness of all communities and states… Injustice anywhere is a threat to justice everywhere. We are caught in an inescapable network of mutuality, tied in a single garment of destiny. Whatever affects one directly, affects all indirectly…Anyone who lives inside the United States can never be considered an outsider anywhere within its bounds.

Due to the urgings of many, Pres. Lyndon Johnson signed the Civil Rights Act in 1964 preserving the commonweal Dr. King spoke of so brilliantly.

My brother Ralph became a career man in the Army. He taught himself to speak Chinese for an assignment in China and learned Twi for an assignment in Ghana. He achieved the rank of Lieutenant Colonel before he retired. His wife, Velma, from New York and graduate of Hampton Institute, an HBCU, served in a stellar manner as the wife of a military professional in addition to her own career in education.

My older brother Arnold drove supply trucks during the war. Barney received the Silver Beaver Award from President Franklin Roosevelt for distinguished service to young people in Boy Scouts in San Mateo and graduated from the University of California, Berkeley.

When Japanese-Americans from San Mateo were interred in relocation centers, Barney was one of the people to volunteer to take care of their homes and property while they were gone.

He married after the war in my mother's back yard patio under white trellises with climbing wisteria vines. His wife, Myrtle, became the first African American certificated faculty member in the San Mateo Community College system.

My father died in the 1963. He was working as a cook at Old St. Mary's Cathedral in San Francisco. His employer and friend, Father Maslanka, gave a full mass in the cathedral for his last rites.

Sometime before his death, my family and I met Father Maslanka at my father's house on Bush Street. He spoke very highly of my father saying that he was a San Francisco pioneer who created a way for many others.

I showed my family the places my father showed us; camping in Yosemite, taking a day's jaunt to Santa Cruz or Memorial Park where I camped with my brothers when I was finally old enough to become a Boy Scout.

Memorial Park was the same then as it was years before: pools formed in the creek were still deep enough to dive in, trees hundreds of feet tall with girths wide enough for five or six people to stretch their arms around, and the soft earth matted with redwood duff, where as young boys we spent the night lying in our sleeping bags under the stars.

Whenever we could, we would visit my fellow airmen across the country. Most of the time we drove across the United States. By this time national chains were building motels along the highways and would not discriminate so it made stopping overnight and finding a place to eat a little easier.

I wanted my children to meet my Tuskegee comrades so they could experience the pride we feel when we're together. These are men who never sacrificed their integrity, who never had to make a man a lesser man to prove their greatness.

I'm privileged to have served under the inspiring leadership of officers like B.O. Davis with imagination to see us as capable men and who brought forth our highest potential with their vision.

Though we probably weren't fully aware of it at the time because we were young and in the heat of the moment, being the first African American pilots in the United States Army Air Corps and excelling beyond expectations opened a door to the future for generations of African American youth to follow.

My story is just one of many, however. I'm honored to be part of a legacy of people fighting for justice and human rights.

Epilogue

These were the days of my father. It seems he was phenomenally lucky time and again as if some benevolent force looked over his life, turning adversity into advantage, downturn to delight. He met famous and un-famous people, and both influenced his life in equal measure.

His story is of the big days of distance, large hearts, and deep creeks: days that you can only dream of now; days when some people's hearts were still whole and they were mostly sane, life was simple and the place was vibrant and clean.

The San Francisco Bay Area of the early 1900's was a pastoral paradise. Edible fish teemed in the Bay and raced up the watershed's myriad creeks to spawn each year. Even the creeks were different then—big enough to float logs, big holes for swimming on hot days—healthier, clearer.

Now our creeks are all filled in: trickles of water search meekly for confluence, making a weak way to the sea. No more fish run up. Things have changed.

In his lifetime my father has seen men of dubious merit promoted to positions of leadership, rules made for some to follow but not others, rogues parading as successful businessmen.

Still his optimism is remarkable and unswerving. His hope lies at the deepest level of personal identity, that which is incorruptible by even the harshest circumstances. Things have changed and they will change again.

Years ago the Tuskegee Airmen had a dream. Their collective dream was a truly American dream; an archetype of dreams that arise out of the muddy swamp of intolerable human conditions.

Their vision was sustained by the heroic words of America's Declaration of Independence that say that it is "self evident that all men are created equal with certain inalienable rights, that among these are life, liberty and the pursuit of happiness."

Through unity, individual determination, and personal standards of excellence, they challenged prevailing beliefs about the ability and loyalty of African American men and eagerly proved with their lives the mistaken beliefs are wrong.

When the Airmen were awarded the Congressional Gold Medal, the president said the Tuskegee Airmen changed America. Indeed they were an impetus for the integration of the military, but these men were not only some of the best pilots in the U.S. Army Air Corps and good soldiers, they are good citizens, and they are good men.